Also by Jim Herrington

Leading Congregational Change: A Practical Guide for the Transformational Journey and *Leading Congregational Change Workbook* (with Mike Bonem and James Furr)

The Leader's Journey

The Leader's Journey

Accepting the Call to Personal and Congregational Transformation

Jim Herrington, R. Robert Creech,

and Trisha Taylor

JOSSEY-BASS
A Wiley Imprint
www.josseybass.com

Published by Jossey-Bass
A Wiley Imprint
989 Market Street, San Francisco, CA 94103-1741   www.josseybass.com

Jossey-Bass books and products are available through most bookstores. To contact Jossey-Bass directly
call our Customer Care Department within the U.S. at 800-956-7739 or outside the U.S. at 317-572-
3986, or fax 317-572-4002.

Jossey-Bass also publishes its books in a variety of electronic formats. Some content that appears in
print may not be available in electronic books.

Library of Congress Cataloging-in-Publication Data

Herrington, Jim, date.
  The leader's journey: accepting the call to personal and congregational transformation /
Jim Herrington, R. Robert Creech, and Trisha Taylor.—1st ed.
    p. cm.
  Includes bibliographical references and index.
  ISBN 0-7879-6266-X (alk. paper)
  1. Christian leadership. I. Creech, Robert. II. Taylor, Trisha. III. Title.
BV652.1.H47 2003
253'.2—dc21   2002013074

Printed in the United States of America

FIRST EDITION
HB Printing 10 9 8 7 6 5 4 3 2

Contents

Preface

In the summer of 2000, Jim and Robert were at Diedrich's Coffee House on Westheimer in Houston, Texas, one of their favorite hangouts. They had no particular agenda, but both were dealing with a head full of ideas. Robert's were coming from a sabbatical he was enjoying. Jim's were flowing from some continuing interaction with area pastors in leadership training.

Robert's sabbatical was an opportunity to focus attention on a study of Bowen Family Systems Theory, an approach to understanding family and organizational life that helped him tremendously. He was able that summer to make two trips to the Bowen Center for the Study of the Family in Washington, D.C., to use their video library and meet some of their faculty. For several years, Victoria Harrison, a faculty member, had been offering coaching and educational opportunities in Houston. It was a foundation for Robert's work in his own family and congregation. As he waited for Jim to arrive, he was sketching out an idea for a book about Bowen Theory, leadership, and spirituality.

Jim was reading and applying family systems thinking to his work in pastoral leadership development, both in the Union Baptist Association's LeadersEdge program and in Harbor Church, which he served as pastor. He was witnessing firsthand the need for helping pastors learn how to make personal changes. His first book, *Leading Congregational Change,* written with Mike Bonem and James Furr, had been in bookstores for only a few months. But already another work was making its way to the surface: a book about helping pastors and lay leaders understand that a congregation is a living system, a book that would help them engage the *personal transformation* necessary in offering effective leadership to their congregation.

Their ideas meshed. Jim suggested they recruit a third member for their writing team: Trisha Taylor. As a trained psychotherapist who worked with many local pastors, the wife of a pastor herself, and a member of a congregation, Trisha would bring unique insights to the project. She accepted the invitation, and the team began its work.

It is our hope that pastors and congregational leaders find this work a stimulus for seeing themselves, their families, and their congregations in a fresh way. But more than that, we pray that leaders discover here both the motivation and the tools for undertaking the lifelong journey of transformation called discipleship. May God's Holy Spirit make the life of the Son evident in his church, that the world may see God's glory!

Jim, Robert, and Trisha
Advent 2002

Acknowledgments

An amazing thing is happening in Houston. Although the city is large, dynamic, and highly complex, a community of pastors and ministry leaders is emerging with a shared vision for the transformation of our city. It is our privilege to be a part of that community and to find a profound sense of blessing there.

We are grateful to many people who share the journey with us and who have contributed to the development of this book. Though we take full responsibility for the content of the manuscript, this is truly an effort of the learning community in which we participate. Although it is impossible to name all of that community's participants, we do want to recall several people by name. They read and reread the manuscript, or they allowed us to look over their shoulders and into their hearts as they served local congregations and lead local ministries.

First, to our congregations, Harbor Church, University Baptist Church, and Clear Lake Baptist Church, we say thank you for your love and support.

We offer our deepest appreciation to our reading team: Tom Billings, Bill Blackburn, Galen Blom, Steve Capper, Jerry Edmonson, Brian Gowan, Suzette Harrel, Raymond Higgins, Robert Hughes, Chad Karger, Susan Lanford, Laura Seals, Gwen Sherwood, Ken Shuman, John Starr, and Kerry Wood. We want to express a special word of thanks to Dave Peirce, whose editorial suggestions were extremely helpful.

Victoria Harrison is a member of the faculty at the Bowen Center in Washington, D.C. Her work in teaching and coaching in Houston has had significant impact on this project, both directly and indirectly.

Our friends at Leadership Network and Jossey-Bass have been terrific partners. We offer a special word of thanks to Sheryl Fullerton and Naomi Lucks from Jossey-Bass for their guidance, patience, and support. The book would not have happened without Carol Childress's enthusiastic shepherding from the Leadership Network team. And to Bob Buford, whose visionary leadership contributes significantly to the reshaping of the church in this nation, we are deeply grateful for encouragement in this project.

Finally, we would like to thank the many pastors who have privately and transparently opened their hearts and lives to us in counseling and coaching relationships. Your courage inspires us and gives us hope that transformation can come to those God is calling to lead.

Jim Herrington
R. Robert Creech
Trisha Taylor

Introduction

An effective leader—one who can galvanize individuals and groups, and who has the potential to help transform society—is a person who has *the capacity to know and do the right things*. Easy to say, perhaps, but not so easy to do. For most of us, effective leadership is a learned skill.

We've all seen leaders who are at best inept, and at worst self-serving. Inept leaders are hard-pressed to help us find the direction we are looking for, because they can't find it themselves. Self-serving leaders use the trust and authority that accrues to them to help themselves, rather than using it to help find solutions to our challenges. Sadly, this situation is no less true for pastoral leaders than it is for political leaders.

Once, people naturally looked to the pastoral community for leadership. But in the face of today's social and economic challenges, the pastoral community itself is in serious trouble. Just like congregants, the pastoral leader faces addiction, stress, and temptation. Despite expectation and projection, we are really no different from those we serve.

Most efforts to address the crises faced by the pastoral community are built on the assumption that information alone produces solutions to these challenges. Consequently, a pastor may go to conference after conference, filling notebooks with the latest information from the most recent highly successful leader. But without a clear perspective on the nature of the system he or she is a part of, the pastor returns home to the demands of life and ministry unchanged. We talk with many pastors and congregational leaders who have become discouraged and cynical. Although they frequently know the right things to do, they lack the ability to do them.

Our purpose in writing this book is to offer a practical pathway to transforming the lives of pastors and congregational leaders across the country. As friends and fellow travelers on the journey of discipleship, we write with a conviction that profound change must occur in the self-understanding of pastors and congregational leaders, in how they understand their role in the groups they lead, and in the level and quality of discipleship they experience and express every day.

Our conviction grows out of a journey, taken individually and collectively, in the pastoral community of Houston. On this journey, we struggle daily with the difficult issues of *personal transformation*. In this book, we share our own stories of transformation and those of other pastors and lay leaders, as well as the practical tools we have found useful in the process of personal transformation. We want you to know that, although we have protected the identity of those whose stories we share, here are the stories of real people. We hope these stories and tools give you encouragement and a practical pathway to personal transformation for you and others in the pastoral community. In writing, we affirm with the Apostle Paul, "Not that I have already obtained all this, or have already been made perfect, but I press on to take hold of that for which Christ Jesus took hold of me" (Philippians 3:12).

A New Way of Thinking About Leadership

In this book, you learn about living systems: a different way of thinking about leadership that each of us encountered in recent years, and that changed how we see our role as leader. As you likely know, most leadership development processes focus on "leadership techniques," to be used by the leader on those being led. In this book, we go in another direction: helping you understand that as a leader you are part of a living human system of engagement and relationship, and helping you learn to become aware of these systems and navigate them wisely. We offer a focus on managing yourself rather than managing others.

Leadership recognizing that a group of people is actually a living system requires a different way of thinking. To help you grasp this thinking about leadership, we introduce some concepts and terms that may be new to you. (If you'd like an overview of these terms, please see the Glossary in the back of this book.)

This book is organized into four distinct sections. The chapters in Part One ("The Call to Personal Transformation") introduce (1) the problems you as a pastor or congregational leader face every day, (2) the call to personal transformation, and (3) the elements of this inside-out process. We also examine the life of Jesus and reflect on the living systems of which he was a part, observing his ability to know and do the right thing despite enormous pressure to do otherwise.

A living system plays by a set of rules we can see and name. The chapters in Part Two ("Leading Living Systems") introduce basic principles that you need to understand to be an effective leader. As the chapters in this section point out, the keys to employing this approach to leadership are (1) learning to *think* differently about how people in a living system affect each other, (2) learning to *observe* how anxiety holds chronic symptoms in place and keeps people stuck in old roles, and (3) learning to *manage* our own anxiety. All this enables us to handle ourselves more calmly and to lead even in the midst of an anxious congregation.

In Part Three ("Family Patterns"), we turn our attention to our origins as leaders: What family systems produced our usual approach to life and leadership? What role do we play in our current family system? Tools in these chapters include strategies that help to decrease anxiety in the face of a living system's reactivity, and help in being successful in our own nuclear families—a place that is of central importance to our well-being.

Finally, in Part Four ("The Spirit and the Journey"), we join a chorus of voices in holding up the spiritual disciplines as the primary means of hearing the voice of God. This hearing is the crucial resource that guides you as leader to know the right things to do—and to find the courage to do them. An intimate relationship with God is the center of gravity that keeps our lives in balance when the pressures of the system threaten to topple us. We are more likely to achieve the goal of personal transformation if we intentionally form a grace-giving, truth-telling community that surrounds them in this transformational journey (Ecclesiastes 4:9–12). This community includes a coach, a peer group, and a vision team.

At the end of each chapter, you will find reflective questions for self-assessment. There are no right or wrong answers; this is simply a way for you to engage with your journey and be present with yourself. You might consider writing your answers in a journal, so you can reflect on your transformation during the journey.

How to Use This Book

This book is a basic overview of some of the principles of leadership in a living system. It should be used as a primer by pastors, congregational leaders, and seminarians. Although the people in our examples are mainly pastoral and congregational leaders, any person who offers leadership in a living system—a school, a business, a community, a family—can apply the concepts.

Because information about leadership in a living system is not enough, you should begin at the outset to practice using the ideas contained in this book. This happens best if you have a group of people around you who are seeking to master the practices as well. The final chapter of this book addresses this subject in some detail.

If you are interested in learning more about leadership in a living system, please visit our Website (www.leadersjourney.org) for a series of lessons designed to improve your skills.

May God be with you on your journey.

The Leader's Journey

To our spouses, Betty Herrington, Melinda Creech, and Craig Taylor, partners in the journey, for their love and support throughout the development of this project.

Part One

The Call to Personal Transformation

Chapter One

The Need for Personal Transformation

*Do not look for shortcuts to God. The market is flooded
with surefire, easygoing formulas for a successful life that
can be practiced in your spare time. Do not fall for that
stuff, even though crowds of people do. The way to life—to
God!—is vigorous and requires total attention.*
—JESUS, MATTHEW 7:13–14, *THE MESSAGE*

Leaders do the right things. Managers do things right.
—BURT NANUS AND WARREN BENNIS

Over the years, we have walked intimately with pastoral leaders
from a variety of denominations and cultures in our city and across
the country. Far too many are fatigued and spiritually empty. The
day-to-day stress of managing an institutional church—small or
large—robs them of their personal spiritual vitality. In this condition, they simply cannot provide the effective leadership required
to lead a congregation down a path of change.

Stories from the Trenches

Kenneth was the forty-seven-year-old pastor of a forty-two-year-old
urban congregation. He held a Ph.D. from a seminary in his
denomination. He served as a graduate assistant in seminary and
as associate pastor in two previous congregations before coming to

his current assignment. About seven months into his tenure, he called me (coauthor Jim Herrington) and said: "I'm stuck and I'm embarrassed. I have all the formal education our denomination provides, and I cannot get our congregation off dead center. I've read the leadership books. I know the concepts. But, as I've tried to lead this congregation to reach its community, we seem to stay in a constant state of conflict. Sometimes the conflict is public and intense. Other times it's behind the scenes and less focused. And I seem incapable of stopping it."

Over several weeks of conversation, I learned that Kenneth had grown up in a highly conflicted family. Caught between warring parents, he often found himself in the middle, attempting to keep the peace. Although Kenneth knew this part of his history and was aware that it affected his leadership style, he was unable to change how he managed the conflict in his church. He asked, "Will my congregational ministry always be controlled by the dynamics of conflict that I learned as a child?"

I (Jim) noticed this perspective in a focus group with twelve Southern Baptist pastors. They were African American, Anglo, Chinese, Hispanic, and Vietnamese, ranging in age from thirty-one to sixty-four. The group was asked, "What is your denomination doing that helps you?" Several pastors gave polite answers, before Dave, a fifty-one-year-old pastor, got to his feet to respond: "Your question angers me. You have no clue what my life is like and you presume that anything you do helps me in my world."

He then went on to talk about his life. He described how he left seminary with a resolve to call people to the life of Jesus, helping them to learn to follow Christ. He described how his hope of fulfilling that calling slowly died and was replaced by the daily grind of institutional maintenance and by codependent personal relationships.

The longer he talked, the more impassioned he became. As he concluded his comments, his voice softened, and tears welled up in his eyes. He said in words that were barely audible: "I'm working harder than I've ever worked, for less results than I've ever gotten. My health is failing, my family is falling apart, and I don't know what to do."

In 1997, we (Robert Creech and Jim) participated in initiating a weeklong leadership development process for sixteen pastors.

During the day we taught leadership skills, and at night we worshiped together. Following each evening worship experience, we divided into groups of five to debrief the day and pray for one another. Much to our surprise, the first night the groups stayed together until nearly midnight. As the week unfolded, several pastors came to us to report their experience in the groups.

One of the participants, Evan, said, "I told my group last night that my wife and I are about to drown in credit card debt." Another said, "For nearly four months, I've been engaged in an intensive conflict with my elders. It's killing me, and I've been so alone. I shared that struggle with my group last night and found such grace and relief."

Yet another, Austin, came to me (Jim) and said, "I want to talk with you. For three nights in a row, I've been talking with my group. They've insisted that I come to you." After some hesitation he continued. "This is hard to say, but my wife and I are in trouble. We've been married eleven years, and I love her deeply. She loves me too. But I have such a temper. Sometimes I get so angry." He paused. "I haven't ever hit her, but often I grab and shake her. It hasn't happened for a long time. Then it happened again last week, and she threatened to leave me."

Austin began to weep. I stood silently with a hand on his shoulder as he grieved his own failure and expressed his fear for their future. We talked about places he could get the help he needed, and we made a commitment to be accountable to one another throughout the days ahead.

These stories are a sample of our experiences and, we believe, are common among people of all kinds. They illustrate things we all know but frequently refuse to say. A recent survey by *Christianity Today* (www.christianitytoday.com) revealed that four in ten pastors have visited a pornographic Website. More than one-third has done so in the past year. Those statistics are startling.

The pastoral community is in trouble. Pastors are called on to lead, but they face the same challenges that every other believer faces. Although expected to assist others in their *personal transformation,* the pastor often has no place to turn for the encouragement and mentoring required for his or her own spiritual formation.

As we talk with pastors and lay leaders, they often ask, "Yes, but where can I get the help I need?" What if someone asks you that question? How you answer is determined in part by what you believe about how transformation occurs.

Beliefs About Personal Transformation

Coming face to face with the fact that many in the pastoral community are in trouble has served to clarify our beliefs about personal transformation. These convictions have been tested in the crucible of life, where change is taking place. As we mentor pastoral leaders and guide groups in leadership development, these beliefs form the essence of much of our guidance. We find these beliefs reflected in and modeled by the life of Jesus.

Our beliefs are threefold:

1. Personal transformation happens best as an inside-out process of committing to obey Christ.
2. Personal transformation happens best in the context of a loving community that extends grace and truth.
3. Personal transformation happens best when we develop a reflective lifestyle.

Each belief is essential because personal transformation occurs when a leader holds the three in dynamic tension. Figure 1.1 reflects this process.

Let's take a closer look.

An Inside-Out Process of Commitment to Obedience

Personal transformation happens best as an inside-out process. This assertion may seem obvious, but we often seek to change our lives by focusing only on the external things demanding change; we blame other people when things do not go well. This reaction is hard-wired into the human species. When confronted with their sin in the garden, Adam and Eve both sought to deflect responsibility (Genesis 3:8–13).

But we're talking about more than just taking personal responsibility. Individuals often take personal responsibility but redouble their efforts at what they are already doing. If you keep doing what you've been doing, you'll keep getting what you've been getting.

Figure 1.1. The Threefold Process of Personal Transformation.

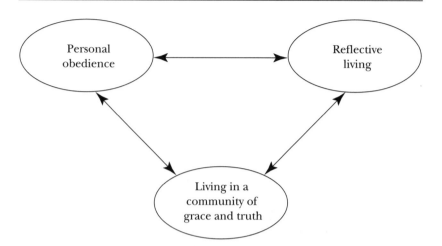

If what we are doing is producing our current results, then working harder at the same thing is going to produce more of the same undesired results!

Here is a story that illustrates both the human tendency to refuse personal responsibility and to redouble one's efforts in ineffective problem-solving actions. My (Jim's) mother taught me this pair of truths in a powerful way many years ago. My older daughter, Emily, was two years old. We were visiting my parents for a weekend and, as two-year-olds will do, Emily consistently and persistently disobeyed me throughout the day. Each time she disobeyed, I corrected her. Her disobedience persisted, so I worked harder in an attempt to get Emily to behave. I viewed her as the problem and continued to attempt to change her behavior rather than act to change mine.

Toward the end of the day, Mom said, "What are you wanting her to do?" After I described the desired behavior, Mom asked, "Is what you are doing getting you what you want?"

"No, I guess it isn't," I said.

"Then why do you keep doing it?" my mother asked with the gentleness of a master teacher.

That has become a parable of my life. When my circumstances do not match my desires, I tend to focus on the external problem and intensify my habitual behavior in the hope of producing some other result.

My mother, and many wise teachers since then, have taught another response. If we are to have an impact on our world, success will come from changing our own behavior. We have the most control over ourselves. Focusing on ourselves affirms that we influence and are influenced by the interaction of the complex systems in which we live.

This emphasis on changing ourselves fits our understanding of God's plans, as shown paradoxically in 2 Chronicles. After the people of God celebrated the completion of the Temple, Solomon had a powerful encounter with God. God knew that this great success would tempt Judah to depend upon external things (in temples then; in buildings and budgets today). When they, or we, succumb to that temptation, the land begins to deteriorate.

In this context, the well-known words were uttered: "If my people who are called by name will humble themselves and pray and seek my face and turn from their wicked ways, then will I hear from heaven and will forgive their sin and will heal their land" (2 Chronicles 7:14). God says that we have a part to play in what happens. When the world goes to hell before our very eyes, we want to place the blame elsewhere: the drug dealers, the school system, humanistic thinking, the Supreme Court, taking prayer out of the schools, inept politicians. But God challenges that thinking. "Do not look to external symptoms," he says. "Look at your own life. Look at your own responsibility. Look at how you have contributed to the circumstances around you, and hear my call to the radical repentance that results in your own personal transformation."

A Community of Grace and Truth

Personal transformation happens best in the context of a loving community that extends grace and truth. The Gospel of John proclaims: "The Word became flesh and made his dwelling among us. We have seen his glory, the Glory of the One and Only, who came from the Father, *full of grace and truth*" (John 1:14; emphasis ours). Personal transformation happens best when the individual is offered a grace-filled environment. When Jesus encountered Thomas's doubt following his resurrection, he did not lash out in anger. He responded with grace (John 20:27). Judgment, criticism, guilt, or shame can produce short-term change, but meaningful, long-term, inside-out change is nurtured by grace. Creating an environment where an individual experiences acceptance in spite of failure allows personal transformation to take root.

Brad and I (Jim) were friends for several years. He was an affable, engaging man who appeared to be a healthy, successful pastor. He joined our leadership development process and was assigned to the peer group that I facilitated. In the peer-group experience, one pastor told his story each night. Several of the men demonstrated a striking honesty and vulnerability. On the second night, one of the pastors wept as he told a particularly painful part of his story.

The next day, Brad saw me during one of the breaks.

"That was some meeting last night," he said. "Lonny really got honest with us, didn't he?"

"Yes," I replied, "he did."

"I'll never be able to cry in a group like that. I haven't cried since I was nine years old."

"That's OK. The goal is not for you to cry. It's just for you to be honest."

Brad's turn to share came on the last evening. As his story unfolded, he related a frightening series of experiences of family violence between his mother and father, who was a pastor. After each outburst, his dad personally threatened him: "If you tell anyone what happened here tonight, I will lose my job."

For years, Brad faithfully hid the family violence. He revealed it for the first time in the peer group, and as he did he expressed years of profound anger toward his father. Powerful sobs racked his body as group members waited. Then the shame kicked in.

"I know it's wrong for me to feel this way toward my dad. I'm sorry. I know the Bible calls me to honor my father and mother. But those experiences were like living in hell, and I've never recovered from their impact. Every now and then, something happens to trigger the anger. I lash out at my wife or my kids. But then I go back to pretending that it's not there. I feel so hopeless. Please don't judge me."

Please don't judge me. This is the unspoken plea that so many pastors carry in the hearts. Their experience may not be as intense as Brad's, but the world in which they minister continually places unrealistic expectations on them. They are vulnerable people who experience pain and struggle. Yet they suffer in silence, for fear of being perceived as weak or not qualified for their calling. They long for a place that is filled with grace—a place where they can be transparent about their lives and the challenges they face. This crucial longing must be met for personal transformation to occur.

But grace is not enough. In the context of that grace, truth must also be spoken. The Apostle Paul tells us to "speak the truth in love" (Ephesians 4:15). Change becomes possible only when we face the truth. Even though we recognize that this truth can be revealed in many ways, we have found the context of the peer group and the guidance of an effective coach to be powerful places of disclosure and discovery.

As Brad's peer-group experience unfolded over the next few months, he was encouraged to explore how his family-of-origin experience was playing out in his life. As the trust among the group grew, Brad became more and more candid.

Over time, he began to connect these experiences and his eating habits (he was about forty pounds overweight). He also began to acknowledge that in response to his father's sin, he had sinned in return. He had allowed his father's failure to fester in his heart. He became angry, even bitter. He lived out that bitterness in a variety of relationships in his life.

With the group's encouragement and with the wise guidance of his coach, Brad began to face the truth about himself and his estranged relationship to his dad.

As a result, he began to visit his dad regularly. Even though his father neither asked forgiveness nor acknowledged his responsibility for the relationship, Brad began to find freedom. He found that it was increasingly possible to relate to his father on the basis of his own principles rather than his father's actions. Focusing on changing his own behavior rather than attempting to change his dad produced dramatic progress for Brad.

In the last peer-group meeting, he said, "I cannot thank you enough for all that you've done for me. I would never have told my story in any other setting. And I would not be experiencing this new freedom if you hadn't accepted me and held me accountable to face the truth at the same time. My life has been changed."

A Reflective Lifestyle

Personal transformation happens best in the context of a reflective lifestyle. The classic disciplines of the Christian faith—worship, solitude, fasting, prayer, silence, and study—are essential to the formation of Jesus' character in our lives. We join a growing number of voices (Richard Foster, *Celebration of Discipline;* Douglas Rumford, *SoulShaping;* Dallas Willard, *Hearing God* and *The Spirit of the Disciplines;* and others) acknowledging that our mechanistic worldview has resulted in the compartmentalization of these disciplines. Marginalizing these practices robs them of power in our lives.

Rather than living a reflective life characterized by the classic spiritual disciplines, far too often we live a frantically busy life that occasionally has daily quiet time. As we try to get some control over all the things that pull at us, God is assigned to the "spiritual" or "Sunday" part of our lives, rather than permeating all that we do. Consider: Do you have a prayer life, or a life of prayer? Occasions of fasting, or a lifestyle of fasting? Do you relegate Jesus to a quiet-time encounter early in the morning, or engage in a reflective lifestyle that seeks to know Jesus' presence in every moment of the day?

Danny is a pastor and participant in our leadership development process. Danny and I (Jim) met one morning to pray, taking turns as the Spirit prompted us. At one point, Danny began to pray for some key leaders in his congregation: "Lord, I confess that I do not love these people." He confessed the long-standing sense of anger and frustration that characterized his relationship to these leaders. He asked for God's forgiveness and then asked God to change his heart.

Danny and I continued to converse throughout the week about his prayer. He asked, "How do I learn to love these people?" As I sought to understand more about his circumstances, Danny told me he felt consumed by the daily demands of ministry. In an urban congregation averaging 220 in worship attendance, he often worked sixty or more hours each week. The demands of preaching, pastoral care, and administration often overwhelmed him. His only encounter with the Bible came as he prepared to preach and teach. He rarely had a long period of quiet reflection. In the stress of his work, he had also developed a pattern of neglecting his relationship with his wife and sixteen-year-old daughter.

For several months following that conversation with Danny, I informally surveyed some of the pastors I knew. In dozens of conversations with pastors in a variety of settings, it became clear that Danny's experience was common. Ongoing spiritual formation was either nonexistent or so compartmentalized that it had little impact in their lives.

Personal transformation comes when our relationship with God is not just one part of our lives. Personal transformation is fueled when Jesus becomes a dynamic, ongoing presence every moment we live. Integrating the classic disciplines of Christianity into our hours, days, and weeks fosters this kind of relationship. Leaders must develop the capacity to set boundaries on the things that drain their vitality and establish space for the things that nourish the soul and renew the mind. Personal transformation happens best when a grace-giving, truth-telling community of accountability supports us in developing a reflective lifestyle.

A Call to Personal Transformation

In all of this, there is good news and bad news. The bad news is that the church and many of its leaders are in trouble. The good news is that God calls us to personal transformation and promises to empower it. Paul declares, "Now to him who is able to do immeasurably more than all we ask or imagine, according to his power that is at work within us, to him be glory in the church through Jesus Christ throughout all generations" (Ephesians 3:20–21).

He is able. But will we allow his power to be at work within us for an ongoing, life-changing process of transformation that allows the very life of Jesus—the mind of Christ—to be lived in and through us?

If you respond to that challenge with a ringing "Yes!" then your next thought, inevitably, is to ask, "How?" In the chapters that follow, we use the life of Jesus and the conceptual framework of living systems to guide you on the journey of personal transformation. Your journey will take you on a practical, proven pathway that has been tested in our own lives and in the lives of the pastors and leaders we serve.

Remember: personal transformation—becoming an effective spiritual leader—is an inside-out process of growing obedience to

Christ. It is helped along by the presence of a safe community of coaches and peers who offer grace and speak truth, but most of all it calls us to a reflective life centered in the person of Jesus Christ. For the sake of your own personal health, for the health of your family, and for the health of your ministry, begin your journey of personal transformation now.

Self-Assessment Questions

- What has changed about you in the past year? the past five years? the past ten years?
- What are your personal beliefs about how transformation takes place in a person's life? What is required for one to experience personal transformation?
- If transformation is to take place internally, what is the role of community in the process of personal change? What role do you think others might play in your experience of transformation?
- As you think about it, what are the key components of a reflective lifestyle?
- Assume for a moment that nothing transformational takes place in your inner life and character in the next ten years. How would you describe for yourself what your life will be like then?
- How would you describe the kind of changes you'd like to see take place in your life? In what way would you like things to be different?
- If you were the pastor/leader that you believe you are called to be (as opposed to being the one that others say you should be), what would you be doing differently? (You can substitute for "pastor/leader" another role, such as wife, husband, father, mother, or friend, and then continue to reflect on this question.)

Chapter Two

Following Jesus on the Leadership Journey

The assumption of Jesus' program for his people on earth was that they would live their lives as his students and co-laborers. They would find him so admirable in every respect—wise, beautiful, powerful, and good—that they would constantly seek to be in his presence and be guided, instructed, and helped by him in every aspect of their lives. For he is indeed the living head of the community of prayerful love across all time and space.
—DALLAS WILLARD, *THE DIVINE CONSPIRACY*

Anyone who intends to come with me has to let me lead. You're not in the driver's seat—I am. Do not run from suffering; embrace it. Follow me and I'll show you how. Self-help is no help at all. Self-sacrifice is the way, my way, to finding your self, your true self. What good is it to get everything you want and lose you, the real you?
—JESUS, LUKE 9:23–25, *THE MESSAGE*

Embarking on the journey of personal transformation—apprenticing with Jesus Christ to learn how to live and how to lead—is what it means to be a pastor in the twenty-first century. Personal transformation in one's own life is the only foundation on which effective leadership can be constructed. To the degree that we are personally being transformed, we are able to lead the way as our congregations change, so that they will be available to God for the transformation of their community. We can find God's grace and power, through personal change, to know and do the right thing.

Every pastoral leader knows the struggle: choosing to know and do the right thing when the pressure to choose otherwise is strong. Jesus certainly faced this struggle, and his example makes clear what this dimension of leading looks like. Let's begin by exploring the difficulty of being able to do the right thing when others are involved.

Franklin's Struggle

"Like a stray dog at a whistler's convention" is how a pastor's life has been cleverly described. We have a strong sense of urgency in the things we are supposed to be about, but many voices beg for our attention. The pull to do this thing or that, to respond to this person's demands or that one's, to give oneself to this effort or that, can be confounding. Even when a leader has a clear sense of what the right thing is, the pressure to do something else or something less can be strong. Given the powerful influence that relationships exercise in our lives, doing the right thing can sometimes be much more difficult than knowing the right thing to do.

Franklin was the senior pastor at College Street Church. For the first time in his young life, he was leading a congregation to raise funds for a new facility. College Street secured an outside consultant to guide their effort to raise $3 million over three years. The consultant, Ray, was a former pastor. He had successfully raised funds in his own congregations and was eventually recruited by a national organization to work with them. Ray was a strong, outgoing, optimistic man with a drive to succeed. He exuded the confidence and charm that made him one of his firm's most productive consultants. His personality contrasted starkly with Franklin's quieter, people-centered introversion.

Ray's advice and experience complemented Franklin's relational style of leadership and the trust he had built with the congregation over ten years. But the goal of $3 million was going to be a stretch for this church, and both Ray and Franklin sensed the anxiety attached to the possibility of a partial success.

When the campaign was introduced to the church's pastoral staff and key lay leaders, one phrase echoed repeatedly: "The senior pastor is the key to the success of this campaign." College Street's young pastor began to feel the weight of the statement immediately. Following Ray's strategic advice, College Street formed a steering committee, built teams to take care of the seemingly endless tasks that were required, and cleared the church's spring calendar to give full attention to the effort. Franklin's own calendar filled with meetings the consultant said were nonnegotiable.

The pastor wanted this campaign to succeed. He faithfully followed the advice and instructions he was given. Franklin enlisted two key congregational leaders to serve as campaign directors. Over a period of several months, he spoke at one training session after another, encouraging and inspiring the men and women who were taking on the hundreds of required tasks. He prepared a series of messages to preach in the final weeks leading up to the day of pledges. Franklin prayerfully readied himself to share his own testimony of how he and his family had decided about an amount to pledge toward the goal. He was expected to share the amount of that pledge with his congregation. Weekly meetings and phone conversations with the consultant kept the pressure on.

One Monday morning that spring, Franklin received the expected phone call from Ray, inquiring about the progress of the campaign over the weekend. The pastor candidly reported that the possibility of raising the full amount of the project appeared less and less likely. Ray said, "We're going to have to do something different." He instructed Franklin to develop a list of the five to ten wealthiest couples in his congregation. The pastor was to schedule a lunch meeting with each; Ray would attend the meetings. During lunch Franklin would outline the importance of the success of the campaign, and Ray would then ask them for a large gift in a specific amount. He explained to Franklin that this often helped people think in a larger amount than they might ordinarily. This would help to ensure the success of the campaign.

Franklin reluctantly agreed, but when he hung up the phone he sensed a tightening in his stomach. He had made it a practice not to treat people according to their wealth, or lack of it. Some of the people he would have to list were folks he had only casually contacted over the years. To single them out now that money was needed seemed disingenuous. The pastor determined to pray about the matter.

Over the next few days, it became clearer to him that, regardless of the success of the capital campaign, he could not conscientiously follow through on this plan. In his thinking, the future of his ministry in the church depended more upon his maintaining a sense of integrity in relationships with the flock than in raising every penny needed for the new building.

The next week, Ray was in town. When he met with Franklin, he asked about the progress made in scheduling the lunch meetings. Franklin told him of the conclusion he had reached. Ray was insistent. The pressure not to do the right thing—as Franklin understood it—was intense. He could sense himself wanting to please Ray and not wanting to let the congregation down. Yet he felt the tension of acting contrary to his principles.

The Human Barometer

We often believe that the great difficulty in life is knowing the right thing to do. Sometimes it is. At other times, however, the difficult thing is simply having the inner resources to do what we believe is right. Franklin experienced a conflict between his beliefs and the pressure to take a particular action. The pressure probably caused him to question his belief for a time. It was a persuasive pressure from a credible source. Consequently, he had to find the courage to do what he determined to be right.

The pressure to conform, to be silent, to explode in anger, to do the "wrong" thing, sometimes pushes in on us like the pressure of the atmosphere. Under normal circumstances, the pressure within us is equal to that surrounding us, so we notice nothing. It is only when we dive to the bottom of the pool or drive to the top of the mountain, where the difference in pressure shifts significantly, that we feel our ears popping.

When the pressure of a living system is so great we feel our ears begin to pop, to resist the pressure requires the strength of emotional maturity that comes through personal transformation. What does it take on the part of a leader to be able to stand in the face of pressure from those he or she leads?

Differentiation of Self

The capacity to take such a stand might be described as an expression of emotional and spiritual maturity. In *Family Therapy in Clinical Practice*, Murray Bowen, a pioneer in the study of family systems, described this ability to know who we are apart from others as "differentiation of self."

Differentiation deals with the effort to define oneself, to control oneself, to become a more responsible person, and to permit others to be themselves as well. Differentiation is the ability to remain connected in relationship to significant people in our lives and yet not have our reactions and behavior determined by them. Differentiation of self might also include:

- The ability to steer one's own course in the turbulent waters of a living system
- The ability to allow the life and teaching of Jesus to serve as one's compass rather than reading everyone else's emotional chart
- Being a less-anxious presence in the midst of others' anxieties
- The ability to take responsibility for one's own emotions and feelings, rather than expecting others to deal with them
- The ability to know the difference between thinking and feeling

A leader who has the capacity to know and do the right thing understands himself or herself apart from others and so is able to achieve distance from a situation and observe what is really going on, without letting personal reactivity or anxiety get in the way. Gaining that capacity is the point of this book. For now, let's simply observe the attractiveness of the life and leadership that Jesus, our Teacher, demonstrated.

Jesus and His Mission

For Jesus, "the right thing" was determined by his understanding of what the Father wanted from him. The right thing was a conviction that dwelt in the spiritual center of his life (John 5:19–20, 30). He lived his life with a clear sense of mission: he was about his Father's business (Luke 2:49). He did the will of the One who had sent him (John 4:34). He defined that mission clearly in his inaugural sermon in the synagogue at Nazareth (Luke 4:16–21; cf. Isaiah 61:1–6). Every other relationship in his life, no matter how powerful or precious, would bow to this one; his own life did not matter to him more than the Father's will (Mark 14:36; John 18:11). Jesus had aligned himself with the Father's plan and purpose; the redemptive mission of the Kingdom had become his mission. This alone determined for him what the right thing was at any given moment. Watching him live out this commitment while under fire to compromise it is a thing of breathtaking beauty.

Determining what the right thing is for our lives or our churches is no easy task. The search requires the engagement of the spiritual disciplines of silence, solitude, prayer, and fasting. It did for Jesus, and it does for us who follow him. Hearing from God is the first step. But having heard, we must still find the emotional and spiritual maturity to do God's will, even when the pressure to compromise is strong.

Jesus and the Enemy

At the beginning of his ministry, Jesus experienced a direct confrontation with Satan (Matthew 4:1–11; Mark 1:12–13; Luke 4:1–13). This confrontation continued throughout his ministry by way of human instruments, including those closest to him (as with Peter), climaxing with the forces of evil allied in his crucifixion. Henri Nouwen observes how those temptations of Jesus remain the essential temptations of men and women in a position of spiritual leadership: the temptation to be relevant (turning stones to bread), to be spectacular (jumping from the pinnacle of the Temple), and to be powerful (compromising in order to rule). The antidote, Nouwen suggests in his book *In the Name of Jesus,* is a life that practices such spiritual disciplines as prayer, confession, forgiveness, and theological reflection. Jesus consistently faced the opposition of evil forces antagonistic to the kingdom he came to establish.

Jesus and His Family

The most powerful source of emotional gravity in most of our lives comes from family. Parents, brothers and sisters, spouse, and children exert a profound pull upon us and can easily become the world around which our lives orbit. Jesus faced that in his own experience. Even in adolescence, he began the task of separating his commitment to the Father's will from the love and devotion he felt toward his earthly parents (Luke 2:41–52).

We infer that Joseph, Jesus' earthly father, died sometime between Jesus' thirteenth and thirtieth years. Mary continues to be a part of the story in the Gospels, but Joseph is referred to only in the past. Jesus, the eldest son, would be responsible to care for his mother and any other brothers or sisters remaining at home. For a time, he took over the work of carpentry that Joseph had practiced (Mark 6:3). This particular spot in his family constellation (eldest brother) must have exerted serious social pressure to remain at home and fulfill his family responsibilities.

When he was thirty, however, Jesus shocked his household with the decision to move ahead in response to God's call on his life. He was Israel's Messiah, so he left home to seek baptism from John and to announce the coming of the Kingdom. This decision must have been made against powerful pressure, from without and within. Jesus would later ask his followers to make exactly the same costly choice (Luke 9:57–62; 14:26).

When Jesus sought out John (a relative) and identified with his message and ministry by requesting baptism, he met with resistance at first. John declined to baptize Jesus, recognizing in Jesus a degree of holiness that transcended his own. In spite of pressure to do otherwise, *Jesus insisted on doing the right thing* (Matthew 3:15).

At the outset of his ministry, feeling some pressure from his anxious mother at a wedding feast in Cana, Jesus resisted the impulse to please her and instead sought the Father's timing in his life (John 2:1–11). Later, his brothers also attempted to pressure him to act publicly. Once again, he refused to yield to that pressure and relied only on the Father's schedule for his activity (John 7:1–10).

When his mother brought the rest of her children to convince Jesus to return home, anxious over his safety, Jesus made it clear that the will of God would take precedence in his life (Mark 3:21, 31–35). He had not ceased to love his family; he had to choose "the right thing," however, despite the emotional pressure to choose something else. He had to act on principle rather than having his decisions determined by others' intentions for him. Once he had accomplished what God called him to do, he took tender action, even from the Cross, to care for his mother (John 19:25–27).

If we assume that the voices of father, mother, brothers, and sisters had no appeal to Jesus, we are probably mistaken. He was able to discern those times when their voices called him in a direction that would compromise his commitment to the Kingdom of God. In those moments, he did the right thing.

Jesus and His Friends

Friends, no less than family, can exert a powerful influence on us, to keep them calm and comfortable when our actions make them anxious. It happened to Jesus. His friends (John 15:14–15) were his spiritual "family" (Mark 3:33–35). Their appeal would have been powerful as well. Simon Peter was especially close to him. When Jesus announced his intention to follow the Father's will, though it meant Jerusalem and a Cross, Peter objected. "Never, Lord!" he said. "This shall never happen to you!" (Matthew 16:22). Jesus, who only moments before had commended Peter for speaking the revelation of God (Matthew 16:17–19), now rebuked him as the mouthpiece of Satan (Matthew 16:23). Jesus heard in the words of a concerned friend the same appeal to avoid suffering he had earlier encountered in the wilderness (Matthew 4:1–11). Peter would later attempt to defend his friend against God's will for him and would again feel the sting of Jesus' rebuke (Matthew 26:31–35; John 18:10–11). Other friends of Jesus tried to "save" him as well (John 11:7–16). Surely the well-meaning pleas of anxious friends exerted a tug on his heart. Doing God's will means at times resisting the loving appeal of nervous friends who offer us another, safer agenda.

Jesus and the Crowds

Jesus often found himself stirred emotionally by the overwhelming physical and spiritual needs he encountered in the crowds that followed him (Matthew 9:36; 14:14; 15:32; 20:34; Mark 1:41; Luke 7:13). The lives and needs of these people held an emotional appeal for Jesus; he cared for them. At times, however, he had to resist that appeal and choose what the Father wanted from him. When they wanted to make him king, he resisted by withdrawing to a place of solitude (John 6:15). This desire carried the stench of the earlier suggestion of the Evil One (Luke 4:5–7).

When the gathering crowds in Capernaum wanted him to reappear in public and perform his mighty works for them again, he chose retreat and a fresh itinerary (Mark 1:35–38). Jesus cared for the crowds, but he governed his relationship to their needs on the basis of principle, not their demands. He would serve them, but they would not determine his decisions.

Jesus and His Enemies

Some social and relational pressures we feel are not positive. Although those who love and care for us can, by their emotional appeal, exert a powerful force to draw us away from doing the right thing, they are not the only ones with such influence. We also experience strong emotional reactions in relation to those who actively oppose us. Exposure to threat (real or perceived) may lead us to compromise and walk away from doing the right thing.

Jesus experienced such opposition from a variety of groups in his life. In general, they were the religious establishment (scribes, Pharisees, Sadducees, priests, and lawyers) and political authorities (Herod and Pilate). From the earliest days of his public ministry, Jesus' actions and words generated hostile reaction from the religious authorities (Mark 2:1–3:6; John 2:13–22). Their animosity toward him increased steadily, until they successfully persuaded Pilate to crucify him. Their threats, however, never dissuaded Jesus from his mission (Mark 3:1–6; Luke 13:31–32; John 10:31–39; 11:7–11). He was convinced that even their threats and attacks were in the Father's hand, and it was from the Father's hand he would take the cup of suffering (Matthew 26:37–45).

The experience of Gethsemane demonstrates that Jesus felt the attacks against him. His commitment to do the Father's will, the right thing, overcame even the anxiety produced by such threats. Through his trial and crucifixion, Jesus refused to allow the pretentious threats of Caiaphas, Herod, and Pilate to deter him from his mission. From the cross itself, he continued to resist their attempts to have power over him. He illustrated his own teaching, loving his enemies, turning the other cheek, and offering forgiveness. To the very end, the Father's will was the wind that directed Jesus' course, not the tides of human opinion and threat.

Jesus Our Mentor

Leaders are not expected to make the journey of personal transformation alone. We have apprenticed our lives to Jesus to follow him. He is our Teacher, our Coach, and our Guide on the journey. He is also our Example. Observing how he responded when under pressure from every direction helps us see what it is we are after.

Your initial response to a review of Jesus' life may easily be, "Well, of course, Jesus got it right. Jesus always got it right. How does that help me? I'm not Jesus." None of us are. We are sinners who struggle to do what is right. We are men and women who yield to the pressure of relationships daily. We often know the right thing to do and do not do it. Sometimes we know a response is wrong, but we do it anyway; Paul described this struggle in Romans 7. The questions to ask yourself are: *How do I get to the place where I am consistently able to choose a response rather than simply to react? How can I grow emotionally and spiritually to the place where I am capable, more often than not, of choosing what I believe to be God's will in my role as leader rather than yielding to the pressures to do something else?* This is the transformational journey.

One caveat: Dallas Willard points out, in *The Divine Conspiracy*, the futility of attempting to direct our lives by asking the question "What would Jesus do?" when we are not practicing the spiritual disciplines that Jesus practiced regularly in his life. Attempting to "perform" as Jesus did when we are under pressure to compromise only frustrates most of us.

Small steps along the journey can produce an effect out of proportion to their size. Consider the impact of small improvements. What do you suppose is the difference in salary between a professional baseball player whose batting average is .250 and one whose average is .350? In today's market the jump in salary would be astronomical. The first player is average; the second would be considered a superstar. But what is the difference in performance? The .350 hitter gets only one more hit in every ten times at the plate, or about one more hit in every two and a half games. The difference in performance is slight. The impact of that slight difference is enormous.

The leader who develops the capacity to resist the pressure of relationships even a little more consistently is light-years down the road of effectiveness. Such a leader, whose emotional and spiritual maturity grows, leads a more effective congregation, made up of people whose own lives are growing spiritually and emotionally as well. We need not expect to be able to do it just as Jesus did. We need only do the things in our lives that can produce such personal transformation, and over time we will see the difference it makes in our leadership.

Franklin's Decision

Let's take another look at Franklin and see how he resolved his dilemma. He decided he would have to take a position with Ray based neither on the fear of Ray's reaction nor on fear of asking some of the wealthier members for a substantial contribution to the cause. His position would be based on a personal understanding of his role as pastor to the congregation and the boundaries he believed he needed to observe in dealing with people.

Ray's initial reaction was negative. He was insistent upon Franklin's compliance with the strategy. But when the pastor held his ground, Ray calmed down, and the two of them looked at other approaches to the problem. Special dinners were held in homes of some of the more affluent members of the congregation. These families proved eager to exercise both generosity and hospitality. Others who had strong financial resources were invited to attend. At the dinners, Franklin had the opportunity to interact with these people as their pastor, to share the vision for the church's building project; Ray tastefully encouraged them to participate prayerfully and generously in the effort. The campaign came within a few thousand dollars of the goal, without costing the pastor his principles. Franklin found in his relationship with Christ the capacity to do the right thing, even when under pressure from other important relationships.

When Franklin acted out of differentiation of self, he was able to assess the situation clearly. As he changed his habitual role in the system, the story played out in a different way. Learning to see and understand systems, and our own role in them, is the subject of the next chapters.

We offer here no instrument or test to determine the degree to which you possess the capacity to resist the forces that would pull you into negotiation over your most strongly held principles. The presence or absence of certain variables in your relationships might gauge this emotional maturity, however. You can roughly judge your own level of maturity in this matter by thoughtfully, honestly, and prayerfully examining your life and relationships in light of the self-assessment questions that follow.

Self-Assessment Questions

- To what degree does the anxiety of another upset me?
- How free do I feel to express my own thinking, to set my own boundaries?
- How much do I depend on another's calmness or happiness to make me calm or happy?
- How well am I able to stay connected to people and take a position when the emotional atmosphere is intense?
- How well am I able to see my own part in a chronic pattern in my family, church, or workplace, and then alter it?
- To what degree am I able to be neutral, refuse to blame or diagnose others, and refuse to take others' reactions and behavior personally?
- How well do I take responsibility for my own emotions rather than for the emotions of others?
- How well have I developed the capacity to step outside the system I am part of and "see" the emotional process, observe the automatic reactions that take place?
- To what degree am I able to regulate my own emotional reaction to others?
- How well am I doing at growing a belief system that is truly my own? Do I have clear life goals?
- How well am I able to express my own beliefs to others without demanding that they accept them, defining my self nonreactively, taking an "I" position?
- How well am I able to stay connected even with those who disagree with me?
- Can I allow enhancement of others' integrity and well-being without feeling abandoned, inferior, or less of a self?

Part Two

Leading Living Systems

Chapter Three

Understanding the System

Systems theory focuses on what man does and not on his verbal explanations about why he does it.
—MURRAY BOWEN, *FAMILY THERAPY IN CLINICAL PRACTICE*

You can easily enough see how this kind of thing works by looking no further than your own body. Your body has many parts—limbs, organs, cells—but no matter how many parts you can name, you're still one body. It is exactly the same with Christ. By means of his one Spirit, we all said goodbye to our partial and piecemeal lives. We each used to independently call our own shots, but then we entered into a large and integrated life in which he has the final say in everything.
—ST. PAUL, 1 CORINTHIANS 12:12–13, *THE MESSAGE*

We've used the term *living system* several times in the first two chapters of this book. By now, you may be wondering just what we're talking about. Whenever you engage in a relationship that is long-term, intense, and significant, you become emotionally connected to one another in a living system. Each person who is part of this interaction begins to affect, and be affected by, the anxiety and behaviors of the others. The better we understand the functioning and implications of a living system, the more effectively we undergo personal transformation and learn to lead with integrity.

In this chapter, we introduce a systems approach for understanding our interconnected lives. Understanding how people are enmeshed in a living system and how it affects both our congregation and us is vital to transformational leadership. The reason for this is simple: *leadership always takes place in the context of a living system, and the system plays by a set of observable rules.* If we are to lead in that context, we need to understand the rules.

Our "Wired-Togetherness"

Our culture's focus on the autonomy of the individual easily blinds us to the reality of our emotional connection to one another as human beings. Although we believe we are acting autonomously most of the time, we are far more often reacting to one another, almost instinctively. We do not even think about it; we just do it. We do it because we live our entire lives as part of living systems.

A flock of blackbirds flies across a rice field at full speed without any organized formation, without any clearly discernible leader. Yet in a fraction of a second, the entire flock can turn 90 degrees without one bird crashing into another. Then, within another few seconds the flock can make a U-turn and not leave behind a single bird. Just as suddenly, the whole flock can "decide" to settle on a power line and then, in seconds, decide it is time to fly again, all in the same direction. How do they do that?

If we can see these creatures as "wired together" in a living system—their flock—then we can better understand their behavior, and ours. The living connectedness of these animals is vital for their survival. If they do not behave in just that way, they perish. So their Creator has invested them with a high sensitivity to one another that allows them to respond instantaneously to a threat perceived by any one of them. They are invisibly and emotionally wired together as a living system.

We human beings do not possess the same high level of sensitivity to one another. We are, however, also emotionally wired together in systems such that we react to one another, often without even being aware that we are doing so. In *Family Evaluation,* Michael Kerr writes that the human family also can be described as an "emotional field." The term "field" is apt, as it suggests the complexity of emotional stimuli that family members are contributing and responding to on many levels. The emotionally determined functioning of the family members generates a family emotional "atmosphere" or "field" that, in turn, influences the emotional functioning of each person. It is analogous to the gravitational field of the solar system, where each planet and the sun, by virtue of their mass, contribute gravity to the field and are, in turn, regulated by the field they each help create. One cannot "see" gravity, nor can one "see" the emotional field. The presence of gravity and the emotional field can be inferred, however, by the predictable ways planets and people behave in reaction to one another.

We can observe human wired-togetherness in a family, workplace, or church. When anxiety rises, we become rather predictable. Our thinking becomes less clear and more reactive. Some of us withdraw; others engage in conflict. We begin to place or accept blame in an effort to avoid taking responsibility for making personal changes. We begin to see ourselves as the victim of others' actions. We assign motives to others' behavior, or we take it personally. Demand for conformity in thinking and behavior increases. We look for a quick fix to the symptoms that develop. The least mature members among us begin to attract most of our attention. Leaders are pulled in many directions and find it more and more difficult to think for themselves. The gravitational pull of relationships has its effect on the behavior and response of each person in the group; the behavior and response of each person affects the emotional gravity of the system.

Understanding this fact furnishes a helpful perspective as we attempt to lead a congregation. To say that we are part of a living system is to say that there are forces at work among us that transcend a naïve focus on the *cause* of a problem (as though any one individual can be labeled as "the problem"). In a living system, whenever a problem is chronic, just about everyone has a part to play in keeping it going.

A Personal Example

I (Robert) frequently encounter the need to learn about the system and my part in it the hard way. As a thirty-something pastor of a growing urban congregation, I was practicing the best I knew of leadership toward change—which, at that time, was not much. I knew some things had to change if the church was to pursue its mission most effectively. I believed I could identify what some of those changes ought to be. As best I could, I led toward those changes by engaging congregational leaders in conversation about the changes, sharing both my sense of urgency and the rationality of the proposed solution.

I had never heard of the systems approach, and I did not appreciate the level of anxiety created in the congregation by the series of changes we made. The anxiety surfaced in the life of Henry, a leader in the church whose own family system was in turmoil.

Henry was a corporate executive. He had two grown children. One, a daughter, struggled with substance abuse; in and out of relationships, she left two small children to be cared for by Henry and his wife. His son, a navy pilot, had been summoned to Desert Storm. At work, Henry was required to lay off a large number of employees. He had undergone open-heart surgery twice.

As a young pastor, I did my best to be present with him and his wife during those crises, and I thought I did a good job. I was stunned when I heard that Henry was calling a meeting of disgruntled older church members in his home. As soon as I got word of the meeting, I reacted in my own instinctive way. Angry and nervous, I gave him a call. He was surprised that I knew of the gathering. I insisted on an invitation, believing I could deal with their complaints, answer their questions, and all would be well.

With fear and some bravado, I arrived at his home that Sunday evening and went in prepared to face a hundred angry parishioners. I found only eight. I listened to their complaints and offered responses. What I could not hear was the expression of fear and anxiety these members of my congregation were attempting to communicate. I was not aware of how much my behavior was being driven by my own fear and anxiety. Instead of being a calmer presence, I reacted emotionally, as did they. The result was that everyone's emotions escalated and the emotional system became even more volatile.

Eventually, Henry, his wife, and four of the others left our church. At the time, I piously regarded that as a healthy loss, since "they" obviously did not share the vision "we" were pursuing. I have since come to regard the experience as a nearly predictable series of emotional reactions. With so many changes in a relatively short time, anxiety and tension had increased in the congregation. That a symptom of anxiety arose ought not to have been surprising. Although there was no way to predict that Henry would be the focus, the tension in his own family life left him susceptible to the growing anxiety among some of his fellow church members. His "immunity" to the anxiety was low, and he came down with the symptom. But Henry was not the problem.

Our congregations are living systems. We are emotionally wired together with our brothers and sisters in the family of God (Romans 12:3–21). Our behavior and choices affect each other in ways of which we are often unaware. What are some of the roots and components of a living system? Let's begin with two key variables: emotional maturity and anxiety.

Emotional Maturity and Anxiety

According to systems theory, two variables work in tandem in every emotional system, governing its function. One is *the level of emotional maturity* of the people in the system and of the leadership in particular. The other is *the level of anxiety and tension* to which the system is subject. The greater the level of emotional maturity in a system, the better equipped it is to handle a spike in the level of anxiety when one comes. The higher the level of emotional maturity, the lower the level of constant and chronic anxiety.

You might think of the level of emotional maturity as a reservoir, and anxiety as the water level. The larger the reservoir (that is, the greater the degree of emotional maturity), the more anxiety it can contain without spilling over and producing a problem for the system. The higher the level of water (anxiety), regardless of the size of the reservoir, the closer the system is to overflowing.

Emotional Maturity: It All Starts in the Family

In his wisdom, God has placed us in families. This is his intended means of caring for us and launching us into life. The most immediate experience of family, of course, is our nuclear family, our parents and siblings. But we also step into this world as part of a larger system: a river that has flowed through history as our multigenerational family. We are both a genetic and an emotional product of the system. In this system we learn about who we are, how to relate, and how to survive. Family also teaches us that the world is a safe place or a fearful place. We gain from family a perspective that leaves us either more or less secure or anxious.

As we grow up in our family, we also develop some degree of emotional maturity. This is expressed through emotional separation from our parents and is described as differentiation of self, the capacity to offer a thoughtful response rather than react emotionally, the ability to remain connected to important people in our lives without having our behavior and reactions determined by them. The family is the fire in which our level of emotional maturity is forged. Eventually we leave that family to seek out life on our own. We leave with a level of differentiation close to that of our parents. Bowen observed that when we leave the family of origin and find a spouse, we are likely to marry a person whose degree of emotional maturity matches our own. We then form a new nuclear family, rear children, and send them out. That is the plan.

God told the children of Israel that their behavior would produce either a blessing or a curse on future generations (Exodus 20:5–6). The genealogies of the Bible, though frequently skipped over in reading, are rich with the truth that God works through the generations of a family to accomplish his purpose and to raise up leaders. The book of Genesis is organized around ten genealogies and is filled with realistic family stories (Genesis 5:1; 6:9; 10:1; 11:10; 11:27; 25:12; 25:19; 36:1; 36:9; 37:2). Even the New Testament opens with a description of Jesus' genealogy and a story about the family into which God sent his Son (Matthew 1–2).

A family operates in a pattern consistent with a few observable principles. Since we learn from our family how to relate, we carry these same behaviors directly into the work system and congregation of which we are part. So does everyone else who is part of the system. Understanding these principles and developing a capacity to observe them in action is an important first step on this transformational journey. It is easier to know and do the right thing if we can be clear on what is going on emotionally for us and for the people God has called us to lead.

Anxiety: Blessing and Curse

Anxiety, most simply described, is our response to threat, whether real or perceived. The response is physiological; it is chemical. It occurs as a result of brain activity that is outside our awareness; we never even have to think about it. Thankfully, we can respond to threat in the blink of an eye. This capacity has been hardwired into our brains and bodies by our Creator.

We experience anxiety in two forms: *acute* and *chronic.* Acute anxiety is our reaction to a threat that is real and time-limited. We react to the threat, respond to it, and then eventually return to a normal state of mind and body. At its most basic level, our response to perceived threat prepares us either to fight for our lives or to run for our lives. In a critical moment when the threat is real, the anxious response can be lifesaving.

With chronic anxiety, however, the threat is imagined or distorted, rather than real. Consequently, it is not time-limited; it does not simply go away.

Consider the importance of acute anxiety. When a child steps from between two parked cars into the pathway of your automobile, very little thinking takes place. Instinctively your foot moves to the brake with the full weight of your body. You quickly check your side mirror and jerk the steering wheel to the left, steering away from the child. Your heart pounds, your breath becomes shallow. You may even have to pull over to the side and compose yourself afterward. But soon, your body and mind return to normal, and you go on. This is a response to acute anxiety.

If you trace the actual physiology of this response, the interaction of hormones and neurotransmitters, you will be amazed by the design evident in your mind and body. So much happens within us in a matter of a split second. When you feel threatened, you are instantaneously supplied with additional energy in your muscle cells. Your heart rate increases, your sensitivity is heightened, and your digestive process shuts down so that blood can flow to the large muscles. Your thinking becomes focused on the threat in a kind of tunnel vision. The threatening event is immediately stored in your long-term memory so that whenever you encounter another like it, you will be prepared to respond even more rapidly. Your Creator has programmed these lightning-quick responses in you for your survival.

Clearly, these responses to threat are necessary to protect us and those important to us. However, not all the anxiety we experience is a response to an actual threat. Much of our anxiety is chronic rather than acute. Chronic anxiety may be triggered in a system by some particular incident or issue, but once under way it develops a life of its own, independent of the triggering mechanism. It continues to be generated by our reaction to one another and to disturbance in the relationship system. Once chronic anxiety hits the system, we live in a heightened chemical state of anxiety that prevents us from functioning at our best and sets us up to escalate additional symptoms of one sort or another.

Unfortunately, as effective as the threat response is in keeping us alive during a moment of crisis, it creates a terribly ineffective state for a person to live in for any length of time. Under the influence of those powerful chemicals, our brain does not do its best thinking. We are narrowly focused and unable to think calmly. We react rather than respond. We take things personally; we become defensive. Such reactions are not helpful to a leader.

This set of anxious reactions takes place in a leader before and during a conversation with a coworker, a committee, or members of the congregation. When we view a crisis as threatening, we are not calm and thoughtful. The chemicals God gave us to protect us flood the body and brain and keep us from solving the problem. Instead, we wound and bruise one another.

Every emotional system sustains some level of chronic anxiety. Ed Friedman compares it (in *A Failure of Nerve*) to electricity flowing through the "wires" that connect the people in the system. In an anxious system, it has a greater voltage. The flow "surges" more easily when the system loses its ability to deal with stress. The anxiety can shock a person through which it "grounds off." Like electricity, chronic anxiety is known primarily by its manifestations. Also like electricity, it is transmittable from person to person, institution to institution, and generation to generation.

Chronic anxiety requires two poles if it is to function. One member of the system cannot sustain such tension alone; a negative pole requires a positive one. Some enabling or anxious feedback is required from another member or another part of the system to keep the anxious atmosphere alive.

To the degree that we are part of a family system that has learned to deal with the world as either a threatening place or as a secure place, we operate in life with a given level of chronic anxiety. We are more or less likely to experience the world as a threatening place. Our congregation behaves in the same way. Some congregations see the world as a safe place to be and are much freer to take a risk, pursue a goal, and respond calmly to crisis. Others see and feel the world as threatening and dangerous; anxiety dominates that congregation. The higher the level of chronic anxiety in a system, the more difficult it is for that system to function in a healthy way. (Later we explore the specific ways in which anxiety operates among us. For now it is sufficient to note that this is one of the principles by which an emotional system operates.)

The Calming Effect of a Calm Leader

Karen sent an e-mail to Kelley, her pastor:

> I would like to schedule a time to talk with you. I am a traditionalist resisting contemporary church. Help! I hope to hear from you very soon.
>
> Thanks, Karen

Once, such a message would have sent Kelley into a highly anxious mode. He would have easily become the positive pole necessary to Karen's negative one, and the sparks would have begun to fly. Old behavior might have included a conversation with the worship leader, in which he would mention Karen's note and his dreading the meeting with her, all offered in a complaining tone of voice. He would delay responding to the request for an appointment, stonewalling her. When she finally came in, he would be defensive and argumentative, trying to convince her how right the contemporary flavor of the congregation's life was.

Fortunately, Kelley was already beginning to understand something of the way his congregation functioned as a living system. So instead of reacting automatically, he paused to think. He knew Karen; she and her husband had been faithful members for almost fifteen years. He recalled that she had dropped out of her usual place in the choir and her role as occasional soloist a little more than a year earlier. Kelley suspected that the stated issue (contemporary versus traditional church) was not the real one. He determined that when they met he would try to think with her through the processes that were taking place, trying to be a calm presence rather than becoming defensive. He wrote back:

> Name the time. When do you get off work? Or would you like to come by here on a lunch break or off period? A Sunday afternoon? After 7:30 on a Wednesday P.M.? Let me know. I'd love to think about this with you.
>
> Kelley

This proved fruitful. Together they were able to describe what was occurring in Karen's experience. A new worship leader, Mark, had been brought in. New people were now involved in the church and in the worship ministry, attracted to Mark's leadership and charismatic personality. Consequently, Karen was not called upon to sing as frequently as before. She began to feel a sense of loss, as if she were not so important. During this same period, her husband's job was requiring him to travel overseas for weeks at a time, leaving her to care for two teenage children. Her anxiety increased.

She responded to the rising anxiety by distancing herself, dropping out of active participation in her congregation. Others thought she was just too busy with her teaching job and did not pursue her. She read this response as further evidence that she was not needed or wanted. Soon, nothing in the church seemed to please her; she became critical about it all.

Karen was not content to remain in that state, however, and took personal responsibility to change by making contact with Kelley. He listened, questioned, and helped her develop a plan of action. The next day, she scheduled a conversation with Mark, the worship leader, to talk about her future in worship ministry. The fact that Kelley chose not to be a positive pole to sustain her negative reaction increased the possibility that Karen would take a calm presence into her conversation with Mark. Karen's anxiety could not be sustained without some sort of feedback mechanism from the rest of the system.

As I (Robert) reflect on my encounter with Henry and his friends (mentioned earlier), I have come to understand that I made at least two mistakes in that experience. The first was thinking I could answer the *why* questions about Henry's behavior, attributing to him and his followers a whole list of less-than-admirable motives. What I failed to see, because my paradigm would not permit me to see it, was that my approach to leadership played a huge role in the whole series of events. Jesus' instructions about dealing with the log in my own eye rather than the speck in my brother's ought to have informed my reaction (Matthew 7:1–5). That the complaints and charges leveled were not the real issue became clear when Henry and his wife joined a congregation that had already incorporated most of the same changes I was advocating. Recently, as a somewhat more mature forty-something pastor, I visited Henry at home and talked with him about what we had experienced together a decade ago. He proved to be most gracious and understanding.

My second mistake was in not thinking through the possible reactions to my effort at creating urgency for change. One pastor I know keeps on his computer desktop a helpful slogan: "You didn't expect applause, did you?" In *Leading Congregational Change,* the authors promote creating urgency as a key role of leadership in fostering change. Creating urgency was one of the right things for me (Robert) to do. However, I failed to recognize that doing the right thing could set off a series of anxious reactions that needed a calm, thoughtful response from the leader.

All of us might have benefited in that situation, had I been a less anxious leader. Such a leader might maintain a sense of vision with great calmness, not reacting to the complaints of those upset with the changes required by the vision. The distress of these members might not disturb a more emotionally mature pastor, not push him to make the calls, worry over the confrontation, or feel a need to answer every charge. Yet he might remain connected to those who level their charges and complaints, perhaps even increasing his contact with them rather than avoiding them because they oppose the vision. In time, many of them might themselves calm down and find a way to stay connected with the congregation and its future.

Leaders who want to understand the context in which they carry out their role learn to pay attention to the presence of anxiety in their system. It is one of the two key variables that determine how well the relationships in a congregation are functioning.

Two Powerful Forces: Individuality and Togetherness

Another piece of the emotional process that powerfully affects the capacity to do the right thing is the interaction of two opposing forces. One force pushes you hard from the inside out, toward being a distinct, unique individual. Another force pushes you just as strongly from the outside, pressuring you to conform, to be part of the group, to lay aside your personal principles and commitments. The effects of these two powerful life forces can be seen in your behavior and experienced in the context of your relationships.

Individuality

Creation is incredibly diverse. Judging from the uniqueness of each of billions of snowflakes and the complexity of the human DNA that makes every one of us distinguishable from the other, we would say that our Creator loves diversity. Paul observes that within the church God has preserved this diversity by gifting each of us differently, allowing everyone to make a unique contribution to the body (1 Corinthians 12:4–30).

We long to express our own God-given uniqueness, to be the person God created us to be, to be responsible for our own choices. We each answer to him for our lives. The desire to discover and enhance that God-given distinctiveness is appropriate; it is one of the forces at work within and around us. In less mature and sinful expression, however, it may push selfishly, putting self at the center of life and treating the other as an object rather than a person. When this happens, doing the right thing becomes impossible.

Togetherness

The other force pushes from the outside in. It is the force exerted by our relationships, pushing us to conform, to please others, to fit in. In its most mature form, this pressure helps us be sensitive to the needs of people around us, choosing to serve them. The same God who created us in our diversity calls us to community (Ephesians 4:1–3). He teaches us a mature love that knows how to care for others without being determined by their demands (1 Corinthians 13).

The togetherness force can inhibit our leadership in a variety of ways, however. Just as self-expression can become an expression of selfishness, the push toward togetherness can become a demand for conformity. Our need for others can lead us to become so dependent upon keeping the others who are in the system calm that we compromise our leadership. The togetherness force can serve as water to quench the fire of our true self, the one whom God created us to be. In our emotional immaturity, this togetherness force is often what keeps us from doing the right thing.

Expressed properly, the togetherness force is an important and meaningful aspect of our lives. We are driven in part by a need to be together, to be alike, to connect—to be accepted, affirmed, and loved. We are created for relationship. The two Great Commandments, on which hang "all the Law and the Prophets," are about relationship—with God and with each other (Matthew 22:35–40). However, to the degree that our decisions are shaped exclusively by this force rather than by our own thinking and acting on principle, our leadership expresses emotional immaturity.

Steve and John: Individuality Versus Togetherness

Let's consider how the interaction of these forces can affect congregational leadership. A good illustration is offered by the story of Steve and John, pastors who were both recently forced out of their churches and who now have new positions. Although they seem at first glance to be operating differently, their experiences are quite similar.

During a retreat, Steve and John gather in a circle with four other pastors. It's the third time the group has met that week. This is the first time either man has openly and honestly shared with other pastors the pain they experienced in their journey through forced termination. As they tell their stories, it becomes clear that their personalities and approaches to leadership issues differ considerably. What strikes the other members of their group, however, is how remarkably similar their experiences are.

Steve's Story

Steve considers himself a "strong" leader. He tells the congregation at Piney Drive Church exactly what he thinks, without regard to how some might react. He insists on a rigid doctrinal uniformity and preaches the final word to the congregation on complex ethical issues. He believes that, as the pastor, he is the head of the congregation and that people are responsible to follow his leadership.

He feels that, like Moses, he is responsible to get a vision for his church from God and deliver that vision to the people. They are responsible for accepting it and making it happen. He calls for personal commitment to the vision, though he often sees only regimented compliance. He sometimes speaks to the congregation in military terms, as if he is their general, leading them into battle. His ideas for the congregation are often good, and the people he leads implement many of them.

The church grows numerically, reinforcing Steve's understanding of himself as an independent thinker and a strong leader.

Other signs, however, indicate that his mode of leadership leaves something to be desired. The pastor becomes terribly defensive and exhibits angry behavior when his ideas are challenged, privately or publicly. Negotiation over differences, building consensus, and compromising are not in Steve's repertoire. It's "his way or the highway."

Several families have left Piney Drive during Steve's tenure. Some are leaving with bitterness over their encounters with him, and they unite with other congregations whose pastors lead with greater sensitivity to the feelings of the members. Some are simply dropping out of participation in church altogether. Others have gradually burned out, responding repeatedly to the challenges and demands of their pastor. Many of those who remain bear emotional, spiritual, and relational wounds from the collateral damage inflicted by the pastor's behavior. On occasion, the pastor's leadership style polarizes the congregation into those who are "with him" and those who are "against him." Outwardly, Piney Drive appears to be growing. Beneath the surface, however, glows the magma of resentment and passive-aggressive rebellion.

When his teenage daughter is charged with shoplifting, some of the rebellion erupts. Rumors surface, complaints multiply, tempers flare, and Steve finds himself the victim of the congregation's decision to terminate their pastor. The issues they rally around include his lack of preparation in preaching, his failure to conduct pastoral visitation, and the excessive time he spends on the golf course. As he tells his story to the support group this week, he wonders aloud, "How can they do this? I don't understand. I've done so much to help the church grow."

John's Story

John views leadership quite differently. He even expresses contempt for the kind of authoritarian pastoral leadership that he sees in many of his peers. He describes himself as a "participative" leader. Nothing happens at Eastside Church unless he has "buy in" from literally everyone. Consequently, little actually happens.

John carefully conceals his own thinking about controversial theological or ethical issues, for fear of dividing the church. Nor does he express his ideas about the church's future, worrying that some church members will not share his vision. He often finds himself waiting for key leaders in the church to take the initiative in setting direction or in beginning a new ministry. These leaders seldom feel the need to take such initiative, other than perhaps to champion the newest denominational program. Really creative ideas are almost frightening at Eastside.

When a creative idea does make it to the table for discussion, all that is required to stifle it is one opposing voice, at which point John ceases the initiative and tries to calm down everyone in the room. The slightest difference of opinion may as well be a shouting match as far as the pastor is concerned. Conflict is out of the question. Peace, harmony, and love have to prevail—no matter what. It is as though John is driving a bus in which every seat is equipped with a brake pedal. It is not that the church fails to make planning efforts; Eastside engages in a process of strategic planning, but the process has stalled repeatedly.

Sometimes the stall is triggered by disagreement on the planning task force. Endless discussions are held and decisions postponed. Sometimes the process gets stuck in analysis paralysis, as the group finds studying the data of their church and community a safer activity than actually moving forward. The planning efforts bear little fruit.

Several families have left Eastside during John's tenure. Some leave with frustration over the anemia of the congregation and unite with some other congregation that appears more vital, whose pastor exerts more dynamic leadership. Some simply drop out of participation in church altogether from sheer boredom. Others gradually burn out, having responded repeatedly to the challenge of doing harder what they have always done.

The mission of the Eastside congregation suffers, as does the morale of the people. They continue to do what they have always done, but with less and less to show for their effort. As a result of the church's decline, the members develop a low-grade resentment and passive-aggressive rebellion. People grow tired of giving themselves to an organization that is planning to go nowhere. Weariness creeps in from seeing their best ideas swatted down repeatedly in the name of unity.

About the time members of the congregation learn that the pastor's youngest son has been expelled from school for possessing drugs, some of the rebellion erupts. Rumors circulate, congregational murmuring increases, tempers flare, and John finds himself the victim of the congregation's decision to terminate their pastor. The issues they rally around include his lack of preparation in preaching, his failure to conduct pastoral visitation, and the excessive time he spends at the lake. As John shares his journey and pain with this group of peers, he asks, still in disbelief, "How can they do this to me? I don't get it. I've done so much to maintain a spirit of unity in the church."

What Is the Systems Perspective?

These two pastors operate with completely different goals and proceed with different means. They produce contrasting outcomes in their organizations. In truth, however, their two leadership styles have much in common. They are both expressions of a low level of emotional maturity that reacts emotionally in its relationship with others rather than responding thoughtfully as a mature self.

Seeing the emotional dependency and immaturity of a people-focused leader like John is simple. Emotional reactivity to the group governs every decision; the approval and disapproval of others is the determining factor in all that happens. Feeling liked, accepted, and loved can take precedence over goal-directed activity to the point of allowing the mission of the organization to wither. The leader's hypersensitivity to the demands, wants, needs, desires, and whims of others paralyzes both the leader and the organization.

On the surface, relationships look smooth and calm, which is the leader's driving goal. The organization, however, operates without the benefit of vision. Moreover, people are so highly dependent on each other emotionally that they cannot engage in the healthy conflict that is essential for any group of people to identify and pursue a shared vision (Acts 6; 14).

The congregation grows susceptible to the anxiety produced by any financial, social, or relational crisis among them, in their own lives, or in the life of their leader. In their anxiety, they attempt to justify and explain the actions they take by focusing on issues such as preaching, pastoral visits, or the amount of time devoted to a hobby. The emotional process is ignored.

When we see things through a systems perspective, however, we find these actions generated not by objective evaluation of the pastor's performance but by the anxiety of the congregational system. The evidence of this is that fixing the particular issues raised does not change things. John can react to congregational complaints by working more diligently on sermon preparation, giving more time to pastoral visitation, and cutting back on his fishing, but the anxiety in his home and congregation will not diminish.

The reason is that in our anxiety we react to one another and then later devise what we call a rational explanation for our behavior. An aphorism in the recovery movement defines *rationalizing* as telling rational lies, and that is a fairly accurate description of our behavior. The supposed content of our explanation diverts our attention from the emotional process that is at work. Alleviating the symptoms does not cure the disease. So, most likely, the congregation's blaming will take some other form, and the outcome is eventually the same: the pastor is out of a job.

A task-focused leader like Steve might contest the thesis that he is operating out of a lack of emotional maturity. From all external appearances, the leader is strong, autonomous, and independent. What is not usually observed, however, is the leader's dependence on others for his or her own functioning.

Emotional dependence on others drives the autocratic leader. Others are there to serve the leader's purpose. The compliance of others makes the leader appear successful; the overfunctioning of the leader is matched perfectly by the underfunctioning of his or her constituency. They are looking for a strong leader, rather than thinking for themselves. The autocratic leader is looking for willing followers who allow him or her to think for them.

Difference of opinion is a threat to be met with anger and to be cut off should it persist. Relationships are distant (when one opposes the leader) or close (when one supports the leader), but always tenuous. The task-focused leader is as emotionally reactive to others in the organization as is the people-focused leader in another system.

The followers of such leaders play their part in keeping the dependence alive. When the leader stumbles in life or becomes anxious, the anxiety spreads quickly to those who are dependent upon him or her. All of this happens in people well outside their awareness. Issues such as ill-prepared preaching, infrequent pastoral visits, or excessive time devoted to a hobby surface as a rational explanation for the congregation's action, which is actually generated by the members' anxiety.

Seeing the Systems Paradigm

John and Steve's stories illustrate leadership types you have likely encountered more than once—perhaps you recognize some of John or Steve in your own leadership style. Their stories reflect the tragedy of the struggle in many a congregation that has left the lives of both pastor and church in turmoil. Leaders often experience the tension of staying connected to the system and offering responsible leadership without being done in by it. Leaders struggle with finding a way to disengage the system sufficiently to foster their own personal health and growth, without cutting off from the congregation the person is called to lead. The challenge is always to stay in the system yet do the right thing.

Effective leadership comes from someone with enough emotional maturity to call a congregation to discern and pursue a shared vision, to remain connected with those who differ with the leader or the majority, and to remain a calm presence when the anxiety rises. This represents a model of leadership demonstrated by both Jesus and the earliest leaders of the Church. Such leadership requires learning to understand the principles by which a living system operates and the context in which we exercise our role as leader. The presence of chronic anxiety and the tension between the forces of individuality and togetherness are key variables in how the system functions.

Such leadership requires a maturity that comes through practicing disciplines that allow one to differentiate self from important others without attempting to control them, cutting off from them, or being determined by them. In other words, we leaders can deliberately incorporate some actions into our lives that over time radically shape how we are able to relate to those we lead. It is possible to lead without controlling. It is also possible to learn to resist the demands to surrender vision and principle without giving up our connection to those who exert the pressure.

I (Robert) recall the anxiety I felt as I opened the box that contained my first computer in the early 1980s. It contained pieces I did not recognize and could not name. But if I were going to put this system together and unleash its power to help me accomplish my tasks, I was going to have to learn.

The same is true for the powerful emotional systems to which you belong. Unpacking the box and being able to match the various components of the system with their names—anxiety, reactivity, maturity, the togetherness force, and the individuality force—this is a good beginning. But if you want to harness the power inherent in a living system, if you desire to grow in the capacity to lead without compromising your principles, you must learn to see your world anew—with a systems paradigm. You must learn to be able to see what is going on around you, observe the anxiety, note your own part in it, and manage yourself amid the pressure. You need to learn the skill of "thinking systems and watching process," which is the subject of the next chapter.

Self-Assessment Questions

- How would you describe in your own words the difference between acute and chronic anxiety? Can you give an illustration of each?
- How would you argue for the necessity of anxiety in our lives? What are the dangers it raises?
- How would you describe the family system you emerged from, in regard to the level of chronic anxiety? Were you led to think of the world as basically secure or basically threatening? What did people in your family fret over?

- How would you describe the congregational system you are engaged in, in regard to the level of chronic anxiety? Do leaders in the system see the world about them as threatening? Are there frequent emergencies and crises? When a crisis occurs, does the leadership take it in stride and solve the problem, or are they likely to develop symptoms?
- How would you argue for the necessity of the togetherness force in our lives? What are the dangers it raises?
- How would you argue for the necessity of the individuality force in our lives? What are the dangers it raises?
- What is the difference, in your thinking, between taking responsibility and accepting blame?
- What are the terms in this chapter that are giving you the most difficulty?

Chapter Four

Thinking Systems, Watching Process

Thinking systemically has always been natural to chess champions. Only the most unsophisticated football fans reserve their praise for the ball carrier alone, or blame the quarterback every time he gets "sacked." In meteorology, it has long been recognized that for a tornado to come into existence, the temperature, the barometric pressure, and the humidity all must reach certain thresholds in the atmosphere at exactly the same time.
—ED FRIEDMAN, *GENERATION TO GENERATION*

But the Israelites acted unfaithfully in regard to the devoted things; Achan . . . took some of them. So the LORD's anger burned against Israel.
—JOSHUA 7:1, NIV

In the last chapter, we introduced two variables that govern the behavior of a living system: the level of emotional maturity and the level of chronic anxiety. We can't observe these variables directly, but when we learn to "think systems" and "watch process," we can learn to observe the indicators of both in an emotional system.

Thinking Systems, Watching Process

The first step toward mature leadership is learning to *think in a different way* about how people in a living system affect each other. This way of thinking requires learning to recognize how anxiety holds chronic symptoms in place, and how each person in the system has a role to play in keeping things in balance. This is called thinking systems (that is, thinking from a systems point of view). It requires the leader to surrender the thoroughly ingrained tendency to accept cause-and-effect thinking, diagnose people, and place blame. Leaders often work in just this way, identifying the problem as "out there"—in the external environment or in the behavior of people within the organization. This kind of linear, cause-and-effect thinking keeps them from seeing their own part and leaves them virtually powerless to effect change, since changing others is ultimately impossible.

Learning to think systems means learning to ask and answer two questions: "What is my role in keeping this problem in place?" and "How can I change my role?" Thinking that the problem is out there somewhere actually *is* the problem. An old proverb has it that insanity is doing the same thing over and over again, while expecting some other result. Another version affirms that if you keep doing what you've been doing, you'll keep getting what you've been getting. From a systems perspective, one might put it this way: "The system is perfectly designed for the present results." Someone has to take the lead in changing the system by learning to respond to anxiety rather than react to it. Someone has to think systems and watch the process.

The second step in being able to respond differently is *the ability to see what is happening with clarity.* Objective observation of the emotional processes at work in the system is a major change in itself. In an anxious system, the leader tends to join others in focusing on symptoms (the complaints and problems) rather than process (the systemic issues and reactions that keep a problem in place.) The symptoms, problems, issues, and people in the system get the attention of those who are unable to think systems. This second step is watching process, the ability to see the emotional processes as they play out.

Seeing the Nervous Water: A Fish Story

My wife, Melinda, and I (Robert) enjoy fishing. In 1998, our church staff gave us a generous gift for Christmas. They arranged for us to travel to South Texas and experience a guided fishing trip in the Laguna Madre, a beautiful, pristine bay off South Padre

Island. This was a different kind of fishing trip, however. We knew what it was like to fish in the surf or in a bay with spinning rigs, using live or artificial bait. What we faced was a fly-fishing trip, using equipment we had never touched before.

We met Kenny Brewer, our guide, one Wednesday afternoon on the beach and had our first-and-only fly-casting lesson. He assured us that if we could learn to cast the line forty feet with reasonable accuracy, we could catch fish. The wind was stiff and Kenny was patient, but we were frustrated. Finally, we met his requirements. He arranged to pick us up early the next morning for our expedition.

This new way of fishing was not just about unfamiliar casting skills. It also involved a whole new way of seeing. Our experience had been in fishing blind: casting out bait or a lure to a likely place and hoping for a strike. When we went out with Kenny, we were going to learn to fish by sight, not by faith! We waded into crystal-clear, ankle-deep water and began to search for fish.

We were not long in the water before Kenny pointed and said, "Look! About sixty yards out at one o'clock. There's a red fish swimming across our path. Do you see it?"

"No."

"Right there. See the nervous water?"

"No. What's nervous water?"

"Never mind. He's gone. Nervous water is when the surface of the water looks different in one place than in the water that surrounds it. You'll learn to see it."

That dialogue was repeated several times during the day. Eventually, we could spot nervous water with the best of them. But it required a new way of seeing what we had been looking at for years.

A new capacity for seeing the nervous water of an emotional process can be learned (a coach or a guide like Kenny is helpful). It requires some new categories for thinking; it means practicing some new disciplines and skills. It entails change in how we relate to others, and it demands time and patience. But leadership in the kingdom of God is worth the effort.

The Emotional Triangle

The response we make to life's threats can be understood as emotional reactivity. This term makes it clear that the response occurs at a level of our being that is usually outside of our awareness. The reaction is an instinctive response (like that of birds in flight). We may later develop a detailed, rational explanation for what we have done, to justify our behavior to others. In reality, we are simply reacting in a part of our brain that operates outside of our awareness.

With some discipline and work, we can become much more aware of our reactions and learn to have more say about how they affect our behavior. *Emotional reactivity* and *anxiety* are nearly synonymous terms. Although we are constantly reacting to our environment, in the presence of anxiety we engage a specific repertoire of emotional reactions. Anxiety stirs the nervous water of our family and congregation. We begin by learning to see the nervous water.

Seeing Emotional Triangles

Emotional triangles are the "molecules" of an emotional system. A two-person relationship is notoriously unstable. As long as the relationship is calm, things remain steady. But all it takes is for one person to begin to feel uncomfortable with something about the other, and the relationship moves toward instability. To manage the increased anxiety, one of the two can bring a third person into the triangle.

How this works is so familiar that we usually fail to see it. Fran, the leader of a women's ministry, becomes upset with the church pastor, Virginia, for not attending their annual banquet. Instead of going to Virginia and talking about the issue, however, Fran expresses her upset to her friend Wanda, the wife of the congregation's worship leader. When Wanda engages Fran sympathetically, the triangle is activated, and Virginia finds herself in the uncomfortable outside position. The next time Virginia and Wanda meet in the hallway, Virginia will wonder why Wanda seems so distant. Fran, however, has managed to calm down somewhat.

The more intense the issue, the more people there are who will ultimately be engaged in the process. Triangles interlock. Wanda can catch enough of Fran's anxiety that she carries it home and spreads it to Mike, the worship leader. At the staff meeting the following week there could very well be an air of coldness as Mike brings his infection to the group.

Triangles are the building blocks of an emotional system. When the atmosphere is relatively calm and stable, the triangles are nearly invisible. But they have not gone away. They are merely waiting for the charge of anxiety to flow through them and light up again. By observing the triangles over time the objective observer can begin to see how the emotional process works in a particular system.

It is important, though, to understand that triangles, like anxiety or the togetherness force, are an aspect of human behavior that is neither good nor bad. They just are. Triangles are in themselves neutral; they exist as a part of human behavior. Operating without our awareness, however, they can work to intensify the anxiety within a system and destroy its relational health. The greater the leader's capacity to see the system and watch the process by observing the triangles, the greater the leader's capacity to remain a calm presence and make a difference in the congregation's life. It is when we do not understand what is happening around us that we grow most anxious. Every living system has a myriad of triangles operating interdependently and simultaneously, thus making the dynamics in the system highly complex.

Jesus and Emotional Triangles

Here is an example of positive engagement of a triangle. Jesus called our attention to emotional triangles, and he encouraged us to use them to advantage in maintaining healthy relationships. He said that if our relationship with a brother becomes unstable, we ought first to attempt to restore it on our own (Matthew 5:23–24; 18:15). Should that attempt not be made, we run the risk of dangerous and destructive triangles forming (Matthew 5:25–26). Should the attempt fail, however, we are encouraged to bring others into the matter (form a triangle) with the ultimate design of restoring the stability of the original relationship (Matthew 18:16–17).

Further, observe Jesus' behavior in triangles. He refuses to enter into some, as with the invitation given him by the man in Luke 12:13 who wants Jesus to arbitrate a dispute between himself and his brother over an estate. He chooses to stay out of that one and calls the man to examine his own motives of greed. Peter's attempt to focus Jesus' attention on John is refused. Jesus instead keeps the spotlight on Peter's own relationship to him (John 21:22).

On other occasions, Jesus finds himself in an unavoidable triangle and manages himself within it by maintaining contact with both parties and taking a stand with each of them on the basis of his principles. We can observe this in the triangle with a lame man he has healed on the Sabbath and the authorities who accuse him (John 5), and a similar triangle with a blind man healed on the Sabbath and the angry authorities (John 9). Notice how he deals with the other two parties personally and focuses on maintaining his own position with each.

The Triangle in Congregational Life

Triangles can take a variety of forms in the congregation's life, some of which may seem relatively innocuous. Here are a few common examples:

- We ask a third person's advice or validation in a matter having to do with someone else, creating allies for our own point of view.
- A church member complains to one staff member about another.
- A church leader reinforces his own point of view by quoting others—"Pastor, everyone is talking about the new screens in the worship center and nobody likes them!" "Everyone" becomes the third side of the triangle, aligned against the pastor.
- A pastor listens sympathetically to a wife's complaint about her husband in a counseling session and finds himself incapable of remaining neutral with the man when he encounters him at the Wednesday night fellowship dinner.
- Two members share gossip about one of the youth workers.
- Following the worship service on Sunday morning, as a couple passes by the pastor the wife extends her hand and tells him, "That was the greatest sermon I've ever heard." The pastor does not realize he has just been co-opted by her into her side of an argument she has been having with her husband over an issue the pastor tangentially referred to in the morning message.

Thinking systems and watching process requires us to begin to see these triangles as the anxiety flows through and they light up. It requires recognizing how quickly we are drawn into them and how easily we draw in others.

Like trying to catch red drum on a fly rod, spotting the quarry is only half the task. Then we have to be able to respond with an accurate cast! What are we to do with the nervous water when we can finally see it? How do we respond to a triangle that we find ourselves invited into?

"Detriangling": Staying Connected and Clearheaded

How can you manage yourself within a triangle you encounter? We can offer no simple steps; that would be contrary to systems thinking, which asks us to see life in all its complexity. The key is to work seriously on the disciplines required to become more emotionally mature; no gimmicks or techniques are going to effect change in the system. Change requires serious engagement in personal transformation.

It is the transforming person, not the clever person with a bag of tricks, who affects the functioning of the system for the better. Ironically, if we attempt to get out of the triangle to change the other people involved, our efforts are not likely to work. Our motives only reveal our own emotional immaturity. We are still trying to assess blame and take responsibility for someone's behavior other than our own. However, if we take such action to express more clearly our own attempt to become emotionally mature, we can have a powerful effect on the entire system. The sooner we are able to recognize a triangle as it forms, the sooner we can decide whether, and then how, to participate in it.

Your aim here is "detriangling": staying emotionally connected to the other two players while being emotionally neutral about the symptomatic issue. Jesus' simple response to an anxious Martha effectively removed him from the triangle she was forming to change her sister's behavior (Luke 10:41–42). He called her to examine her own priorities and to allow Mary her choices.

The most strategic role in the system is that of the calm observer. Someone needs to be in the position of being able to see what is going on. Shouldn't it be you, the leader?

As the anxiety in the system rises, so must our resolve to remain composed. As leaders, when we focus on the process we learn not to automatically take sides on the presenting issue. Stay alert; the togetherness forces will become intense, calling for you as leader to arbitrate. Instead you must learn to stay focused on God, your principles, and your reactions. You must also learn to avoid taking responsibility for the relationship of the other two. Only by doing so can you ultimately be helpful.

In *Generation to Generation,* Friedman observed that the more one tries unsuccessfully to change the relationship of two others, the more likely the person is to wind up bearing the stress that rightfully belongs to the other two. Changing the lives of people is ultimately the work of God's Spirit. At times we feel compelled to take on that role ourselves, but to do so is foolish and fruitless.

Dallas Willard describes such behavior as an attempt at control, equating it with Jesus' warning against casting pearls before swine. "God has paid an awful price to arrange for human self-determination," he says in *The Divine Conspiracy*; "he obviously places great value on it." Ironically, we do not make others more responsible by taking responsibility for them.

Moses and Israel are a great example of just such a triangle. In an ideal setting, Moses would deal with his relationship with God; Moses would deal with his relationship with Israel and Israel would take responsibility for dealing with its relationship to God and its relationship with the leader. But these two-person relationships are inherently unstable. So when the Israelites became uncomfortable with having to deal with God face-to-face, they triangled in their leader, Moses (Exodus 20:19). Moses found himself in the stressful position of mediator, going back and forth between God and Israel, when Israel should have been dealing with God personally. Contemporary pastors can easily find themselves stuck in this same triangle!

Gregg and Joyce, two associates on the pastoral leadership team at Northside Fellowship, are often at odds with each other. The issues vary, but the behavior is consistent. Things are quiet for a time, but when tension arises in the church's life, when finances are tight, when attendance is down, when complaints are up, the behavior is predictable. Gregg begins to attack Joyce's work; her ideas are not creative enough to suit him. In his mind, she is the cause of the problems the church is facing. But Gregg never makes these accusations to Joyce; they are always made in the context of a triangle with other team members.

Gregg frequently involves Karl, the senior pastor. Initially, Karl sides with Gregg on the issue and promises to do something about Joyce and her performance. He is triangled. Gregg calms down, but Karl now bears the stress.

Once Karl begins to get a sense of thinking systems and watching process, however, he can see the nervous water and predict the behavior. This ability to observe helps him learn to anticipate Gregg's approaches and to see them, not as the result of Gregg's bad behavior (implicitly siding with Joyce) or as Joyce's poor performance (siding with Gregg), but as an expression of the anxiety in the system. His calmer perspective helps him learn to respond to Gregg less anxiously, sometimes playfully, and push Gregg to work more directly on his relationship with Joyce. It also allows the system to cool down considerably.

Recognizing Chronic Anxiety

How do we human beings typically deal with the anxiety that is inevitable in our family or organization? We have developed a small repertoire of symptomatic behaviors. Four such symptoms recur in living systems:

1. Conflict
2. Distancing
3. Overfunctioning-underfunctioning reciprocity
4. Projection onto a third person

This observation is one of the most insightful contributions of those who study living systems (Kerr and Bowen, *Family Evaluation*). All over the world, in all types of systems, the behaviors we introduce here occur again and again. These reactions become a symptom of the presence of anxiety in our family or congregation. In other words, when we observe the presence of any of these four symptoms in a family or organization, we know we are dealing with an anxious system.

Some systems employ the entire repertoire. Usually, such a system manages to function a little better than one that chooses to "specialize" in just one reaction. When a system specializes, that particular symptom can manifest with great intensity.

Although each of these four responses manages to keep the anxiety spill contained in one place, each also contributes systemically to the level of anxiety in the system, causing it to rise. We are anxious, we react, and we produce a symptom. We become more anxious because of the presence of the symptom. The dance goes on.

Conflict

Conflict is perhaps the most obvious of the symptoms in a living system. Conflict emerges during time of anxiety when togetherness forces combine with all-or-nothing thinking. People begin to insist on their way as the only way. As others disagree, the level of anxiety rises, and the conflict spirals upward.

When it comes to dealing with a family or an organization, we often get stuck in a "medical model." Our cultural paradigm says that there is an individual or group of people in whom the problem resides. We diagnose the person or group as the problem and attempt to change them. Or we focus on the symptom (conflict) and require all hands to receive special conflict management training, learning new techniques to communicate their feelings to each other. All of this is to ignore the nature of the system, whose anxiety produces the symptom in the first place.

Systems theory predicts, however, that if we eliminate the conflict without dealing with the anxiety that produces it, the symptom is sure to recycle itself and show up in one of the other forms discussed here. Our effort becomes a "fix that fails." Contemporary approaches to organizational life, however, do not teach the leader to attend to other evidence of chronic organizational anxiety; conflict seems to get all the attention. But a congregation relatively free of conflict might simply be dealing with its anxiety in other ways.

If conflict is seen as a symptom rather than the problem, we ask different questions. We look at the processes taking place in the system of relationships rather than pointing a finger at the conflictual parties and trying to simply solve their problem.

The apostles took a systems approach in the conflict faced by the early church in Jerusalem. A system problem kept Hellenistic Jewish widows from being cared for, and conflict arose. Rather than dealing with the conflict and trying to get everyone just to communicate better, they restructured the system, putting seven Hellenists in charge of the ministry (Acts 6). The conflict was a symptom. The solution was in the system.

Distance

Some people cannot tolerate conflict in relationships and find another way to deal with an increase in anxiety. As anxiety rises, they withdraw emotionally, keeping the relationships peaceful but superficial. Extreme expressions of distancing are known as "cut-off," in which the relationships are broken off completely. Distant relationships in an emotional system are as much a symptom of increasing anxiety as is intense conflict.

The New Testament presents the church as a community of intense relationships. Believers are called to share life, to practice love and forgiveness as indicators that they are true followers of Jesus (John 13:34–35). The "one another" commands of the New Testament imply that believers are to relate at a level of intensity that results in their offending one another occasionally! Distancing and cutoff make it impossible to fulfill that vision.

Superficial relationships keep conflict to a minimum, but they do not make the anxiety disappear. A congregation in which people refuse to interact at a more-than-superficial level is an anxious system.

Sometimes distance and cutoff transcend the local congregation. More than one church has been formed by the conflict in another congregation that produced a split. It is not unusual for years to pass without any interaction between the members of the original congregation and those of the splinter group. In the late 1990s, distance and cutoff became recognizable symptoms of the anxiety pervading several major denominations. Congregations have distanced themselves or cut themselves off from their denominational roots. This symptom of anxiety has shown itself in strained, superficial relationships between leaders of congregations who find themselves on opposing sides of the dispute. A systems approach does not diagnose and place blame but sees this behavior as evidence of a highly anxious system.

Distancing can show up in a church in many ways. Cold worship services, people falling through the cracks, prayer requests that seldom go beyond the superficial, a problem with retention of new members, passive-aggressive behavior of a church leader or staff member—these and a host of other behaviors may be evidence of a congregation dealing with its anxiety through distance and cutoff.

Overfunctioning and Underfunctioning

Sometimes a system responds to anxiety by engaging in a scenario in which members unwittingly conspire to focus on one person (or part) who seems not to be doing so well (the underfunctioning one). To compensate for this underfunctioning, another member (or part) of the system works very hard (overfunctioning), sometimes complaining the whole time.

This is easily observed in a family. One spouse (the underfunctioning one) may begin to drink heavily, for example. This results in loss of a job, a DWI charge, depression, or violence. Others in the family then overfunction. They take a second job, make excuses to cover up the drinking problem, pay the fine, and accept every promise of the drinker to do better. The overfunctioning members play their part in keeping the condition of the underfunctioning member chronic. Everyone in the system, even the underfunctioning one, agrees on where the problem lies. What they do not see is that the symptom grows out of the relationship system. They do not see their own role in keeping the symptom in place.

Ann and her husband, Daryl, frequently clash over his driving. He has no regard for either the speed limit or the fear and anxiety that speeding creates in her (ten years earlier, her sister was killed in an automobile accident). Ann's complaining has not produced a change in Daryl's driving habits.

One evening Ann and Daryl are taking visiting family members across town for dinner. They are in two vehicles, with Daryl driving the lead car and Ann following. True to form, he is driving fast and furiously, and Ann is doing her best to keep up with him.

Her anxiety is rising by the second. Then it dawns on her: she has a part to play in this silly chase scene. She has her own gas and brake pedals, and she can control them. She is responsible only for her vehicle and those who are with her. She slows down to the speed limit. When she does, her anxiety begins to subside. More than that, she is able to see in this episode of her life a kind of metaphor for how she has played the part of an overfunctioner in many of the chase scenes in her life—with Daryl and others—trying her best to control their behavior rather than changing her own.

In a congregation, overfunctioning or underfunctioning can show up in a variety of ways. We see it in the financial crisis that comes when a high percentage of congregational members underfunction, not giving their part to maintain the church's life and ministry, while a small portion overfunctions, giving more than their share and even increasing their giving when the "summer crunch" hits. It shows up when a pastor overfunctions, taking full responsibility for the success of the church's ministry, reinforcing the underfunctioning of congregational leaders. The dance becomes evident when one member of the church staff continues to perform poorly and others on the staff cover for the under-functioning one, making excuses and doing that person's work, even while blaming the underfunctioner as being the problem. The dance is manifest when congregational members insist on the pastor's thinking for them, or when the pastor insists on telling the congregation what to think. It shows up when the Moses-God-Israel triangle develops—the people of God not being willing to take responsibility for their own relationship with God, pressuring the "clergy" to take responsibility for that. Pastors who become professional holy men or women play their part in keeping the symptom alive. In short, the overfunctioning-underfunctioning exchange is about someone in the system taking on too much responsibility for others.

Projection

We have one other means of reacting to chronic anxiety. Rather than engaging in conflict, distancing ourselves from each other, or taking responsibility for others, we project our anxiety onto one member (or one part) of the system. Again, this is most easily observed in the family. Anxiety that might otherwise express itself as conflict between spouses, for example, is managed by projecting it upon a child. As tension increases in the home, Mom and Dad begin to observe, talk about, and worry over their son's performance in school. They talk to him about it, and they worry over him. They also worry in the presence of his teacher, who then begins to see the child differently. The child grows anxious as these important people worry about him (who would not?) and loses a sense of competency. His grades drop, reinforcing his parents' anxiety, his teacher's opinion, and his sense of incompetency. The feedback system is in place. By this time, everyone has a part to play in keeping the symptom alive.

Physical, emotional, and social symptoms in a child are sometimes kept in a chronic state by just such an anxious response as this. Meanwhile, the marriage looks fairly healthy and free of conflict, since the anxiety in the system is bound up in the *child's* problem.

Conflict or behavioral problems that develop near the bottom of an organizational chart are often a projection of anxiety that would otherwise be expressing itself at the top. Replacing the people at the lower levels does not solve the problem. New people simply step into the old triangle and find themselves eventually replaced as well. It is far easier to diagnose a secretary as the problem, and focus on her incompetence or replace her, than it is to deal with the tension between a pastor and an administrator.

Anyone who desires to think systems and watch process must become familiar with the nervous water of emotional reactivity. Conflict, distance, overfunctioning and underfunctioning, and projection are all evidence that something is going on emotionally in a system that needs more than a Band-Aid. The processes producing those symptoms need to be observed and our part in them changed.

Characteristics of an Anxious System

What does a highly anxious system look like? We have all been there. Ed Friedman focuses on five central traits of a chronically anxious system in *A Failure of Nerve*. These characteristics are not intended to be judgmental, but descriptive. This is how human beings tend to function when their world is perceived as threatening and they grow anxious. An emotionally mature leader who knows how to respond thoughtfully and more calmly can make a difference in anxious times.

Heightened Level of Reactivity

The first characteristic, a heightened level of reactivity, marks an anxious system. The responses of the group members to one another are automatic and instinctive, bypassing the thinking part of the brain and keeping the emotional atmosphere at a highly charged level. People are quick to interrupt each other, think for each other, and complete one another's sentences. Members are as quick to take things personally, as they are to make things personal. The system can easily heat up, with the slightest provocation, over the most inconsequential issue. In this state, it is the response of the system to organize itself around the least-mature member, rather than around its potential leader.

In such an environment, people confuse their feelings with their opinions. Those who tend to become hysterical and hyperactive do. Those inclined to be passive and withdrawn are that way. The life of the group is seldom (perhaps never) marked by objective, dispassionate discussion of issues. Perhaps the most easily discerned characteristic of an anxious system is the loss of playfulness and humor. Everything is dire and serious. In fact, the word *serious* is heard a lot in an anxious system. An anxious system is highly reactive.

The Herding Instinct

Second, an anxious system is marked by an increase in togetherness forces pushing for conformity—the "herding instinct." God values both unity and diversity; the church often finds itself dealing with uniformity or division. The greater the level of anxiety, the more we pressure one another to be the same, to think the same, to conform.

When chronic anxiety permeates the system, the push toward togetherness discourages dissent. Feelings become more important to the group than ideas. The system consistently chooses peace over progress, comfort over experimentation, and the security of the port over the adventure of the open seas. Black-and-white, all-or-nothing thinking marks the system. The overall effect of this togetherness is to create a vicious cycle; as Friedman observes in *A Failure of Nerve*, increased anxiety produces increased reactivity, which leads to increased herding, resulting in increased anxiety, and so on. In an anxious system, the herding instinct takes over.

Blame Displacement

A third trait of the anxious system is what Friedman, in that same book, calls "blame displacement." This is the human tendency to look outward for explanations rather than inward. You can find this response as early as the third chapter of Genesis: Adam blames Eve and God, and Eve blames the serpent. The blame game has been one of our favorite responses to anxiety ever since. Anxious systems do a lot of finger pointing. People see themselves as victimized rather than taking responsibility for their own attitudes and behaviors. Members engage constantly in diagnosing others, focusing on what is wrong with others.

Ironically, this refusal to look inward and take responsibility also prevents people from looking inward to see the strengths God has given them to deal with life. The blame game keeps them from thinking about taking responsibility for themselves.

A Quick Fix

Fourth, an anxious system spends much of its energy looking for a quick fix to its problems. Friedman sees this as the flip side of the tendency to blame others for a problem. Anxious people expect others to solve their problems, and to do it now. Anxious people have a lower threshold for pain and want solutions that are painless. They focus simply on eliminating the symptoms rather than on dealing with those underlying emotional processes keeping the symptoms alive. The door is open for books, seminars, and consultants who can offer how-to's, simple techniques, and "three easy steps." If the problem is systemic, however, focus on fixing one symptom only recycles the anxiety elsewhere. A quick fix is futile.

Poor Leadership

The fifth characteristic of a highly anxious system is that it lacks a leader who operates with clear vision and thoughtfully held principles. As Friedman states definitively, "The fact that chronically anxious families always lack well-differentiated leadership is absolutely universal. I have never seen an exception to this rule."

Chronically anxious groups require someone who can offer a new kind of leadership if they are ever to pull out of their anxious regression. Such leaders are people who can hold on to their own sense of personal vision and principles despite the resistance and pressure of their relationships in the system. They are leaders who can do the right thing. At the same time, such leaders are able to stay in relationship with those they lead, without having to control them or without being done in by them.

Unfortunately, Friedman says, a system that operates without well-differentiated leadership makes it extremely difficult for such a leader to develop. The group's anxiety inhibits the leader's ability to get the distance necessary to think out vision with clarity. Instead, the leader is buffeted about by crisis after crisis. The group's movement toward togetherness leaves the leader reluctant to take a well-defined position that expresses a clear stand on the basis of vision and principle. Under such pressure, the leader become indecisive, not wanting to offend any of the parties. As the blame game gets under way, those in leadership are a prime target for those doing the shooting. If the leader refuses to work on the quick fix that the anxious organization demands, the group turns to others who are less mature. The chronically anxious system is ultimately leaderless.

Part of the arsenal of effective leadership is the wisdom to see the anxiety in the system for what it is, the serenity to take a more objective view of what is transpiring, and the courage to act on principle rather than react to pressure. Learning to see the anxiety as it rises, as the triangles form, as clear thinking fades, as blame becomes the norm, as demands for conformity increase—this is the challenge for a leader who thinks systems and watches process.

Taking Yourself Out of the Triangle

Finding the fish is one thing. Placing a fly in front of it with the wind blowing and the adrenaline pumping is another. We can learn how triangles operate, how to see them, and how to manage ourselves wisely in them. We can learn to recognize the evidence that anxiety is rising in the systems we lead. We can learn to observe the symptoms of an anxious system and to understand the forces that keep them in place. We can discover a wider array of options and responses as we think systems and watch process. We can find a way of taking a more objective, less anxious stance in the midst of the reactivity of others.

As we do so, the system can function better. A calmer leader can emerge who contributes to transforming the life of the congregation. Bowen wrote in *Family Therapy in Clinical Practice* that "when any key member of an emotional system can control his own emotional reactiveness and accurately observe the functioning of the system and his part in it, and he can avoid counter-attacking when he is provoked, and when he can maintain an active relationship with the other key members without withdrawing or becoming silent, the entire system will change in a series of predictable steps."

Jesus said, "Don't pick on people, jump on their failures, criticize their faults—unless, of course, you want the same treatment. That critical spirit has a way of boomeranging. It's easy to see a smudge on your neighbor's face and be oblivious to the sneer on our own. Do you have the nerve to say, 'Let me wash your face for you,' when your own face is distorted by contempt? It's this whole traveling road-show mentality all over again, playing a holier-than-thou part instead of just living your part. Wipe that ugly sneer off your own face, and you might be fit to offer a washcloth to your neighbor" (Matthew 7:1–2, *The Message*).

The process of becoming such a leader now becomes the focus of our attention.

Self-Assessment Questions

- Think of an issue currently working in your family or congregation. Reflect on these two questions: "What is my role in keeping this problem in place?" and "How can I change my role?"
- How would you describe the workings of one of the key emotional triangles you are a part of? Who are the other two players? What typically gets the triangle going? Do you usually find yourself on the inside or the outside during a time of anxiety? If you wanted to get the triangle going, what would you need to do?
- Of the four symptoms of chronic anxiety discussed in this chapter, which do you most typically see in your congregational system? How about in your own family?
- If you were able to see the current issue in your congregation as a symptom of anxiety rather than as the problem, what additional options of response would be available to you?

Chapter Five

Becoming a Calm Leader

*One major sign of being better differentiated is when we
can be present in the midst of an emotional system in
turmoil and actively relate to key people in the system while
calmly maintaining a sense of our own direction. It is
relatively easy to appear to be differentiated when the
system is calm; the test is being able to maintain a calmer
sense of self when the emotional environment deteriorates
and life becomes more chaotic.*
—RONALD RICHARDSON, *CREATING A HEALTHIER CHURCH*

*Don't become so well-adjusted to your culture that you fit
into it without even thinking. Instead, fix your attention
on God. You'll be changed from the inside out. Readily
recognize what he wants from you, and quickly respond to
it. Unlike the culture around you, always dragging you
down to its level of immaturity, God brings the best out of
you, develops well-formed maturity in you.*
—ST. PAUL, ROMANS 12:2, *THE MESSAGE*

You've been introduced to living systems, how triangles work, and
how better managing yourself in your triangles can significantly
influence the outcome of a difficult situation.

In this chapter, we introduce some practical ways for you as
leader to exercise personal responsibility by reducing the anxiety. These are effective means for lowering your own anxiety
and allowing time to gain perspective to diffuse the anxiety of
a system. These actions increase the likelihood of a thoughtful

response that reflects the values and beliefs held by those in the system.

Our suggestions for reducing anxiety and increasing personal responsibility do not constitute a comprehensive list. As a leader, you must develop your own unique repertoire for calming yourself. Doing so makes it possible to have more choices, to be less caught up in the anxiety of the moment.

The Value of Becoming Less Anxious

Nathan is a bright, energetic pastor with an M.B.A. from a private college. He worked in the business world for nine years before responding to a call to vocational ministry, and during his first year of seminary the people of St. John's Church invited him to become their pastor.

The church had a history of serious conflict. During its first seven years of existence, three pastors had come and gone. The church was in a desperate state, and Nathan accepted their call, not realizing or prepared for what he was getting into. Two months into Nathan's tenure at St. John's, warfare erupted. A low level of maturity among the leadership accompanied a lack of shared vision and values.

Virtually demoralized, Nathan considered quitting. He called one day to talk with me (Jim) about resigning. I asked if he had considered any other options.

"What other options?" he asked.

I went on to suggest that he could focus on his own inner life and learn to be a less-anxious presence in this congregational system. I briefly outlined the concepts of leadership defined as doing the right thing despite the system's anxiety, and about differentiation of self. By the time the conversation ended, he said: "I'll make a deal with you. You let me put your name as a reference on my résumé and help me circulate it among pastorless churches in the city. I'll work on understanding this less-anxious-presence stuff and see if practicing it helps."

Nathan did not get any invitations to lead another congregation. But he did begin practicing being less anxious. We met weekly for about fourteen weeks, and each time he would bring a case study from his work in the previous week.

Two days after one of our meetings, Nathan called again. "Help!" he said.

"What's up?" I replied.

"A few minutes ago, John, the newest member of our elder team, came by to say that he and his wife are leaving the church because another elder's wife offended his wife." Nathan paused, and I waited.

"I know you've told me over and over that leadership is about doing the right thing. You are helping me learn to see my anxiety and the anxiety of those around me. But honestly, Jim, there are just times when it's all I can do not to lash out and strike back. This guy makes me so angry. And his wife is worse. Everything anyone says or does offends her. Everywhere they go, chaos follows. It's almost as if the church made him an elder in hopes that he and his wife would be less of a problem. Today, when he came in, I'd had enough. It was all I could do not to tell him to take a flying leap."

"Well, what did you do?"

"Nothing yet. He's in the conference room waiting for me. I got so angry when he started talking, I asked him to excuse me for a moment so I could finish up something I was working on. I came in here to call you. I just needed to calm down for a minute before responding to John."

Nathan learned a powerful lesson. He did indeed do something. He took the initiative to calm himself so that he could be less anxious in the midst of this conflict. The leader's ability to calm himself or herself in the face of anxiety increases the likelihood of a well-thought-out, well-differentiated response that reflects beliefs and values. Although we don't always have the option of asking an angry elder to wait while we call a coach to calm our reactivity, every leader can increase his or her capacity to be less anxious. As Ronald Richardson writes in *Creating a Healthier Church*:

> The leader's main job, through his or her way of being in the congregation, is to create an emotional atmosphere in which greater calmness exists—to be a less anxious presence. "Knowing everything" is not necessary to be a healthy, competent leader. When you can be a less anxious presence, there is often enough experience and wisdom in the group for the group itself to figure out its own

solutions to the challenges it faces. When a leader cannot contribute to this kind of atmosphere, the thinking processes in the group are short-circuited, and people become more anxious and more emotionally reactive and make poorer decisions.

How Does a Leader Become Less Anxious?

How can you, as a leader, participate in creating such an emotional atmosphere? By managing your own anxiety. Functioning as a calming presence fosters more effective thinking and action.

Remember, the goal is not to become nonanxious. That is surely not possible for the human species. What is possible is to learn to be *less* anxious. As one pastor said to us, "I don't have to be nonanxious. I just try to be less anxious than anyone else in the room."

As we noted in Chapter Two, Jesus is the supreme example of the behavior we are describing. Although pressed in on every side from family, friends, religious leaders, and enemies to respond to their anxiety, in each case he did the right thing. Imagine the intensity of the anxiety in the very public encounter with the woman caught in adultery (John 8:1–11). Yet Jesus listened. He reflected; he communicated his values with clarity. Or consider what he must have felt as the rich young ruler walked away from his invitation to life (Matthew 19:16–22). Yet Jesus resisted the temptation to persuade or convince. As nails were driven into his body, he did not even succumb to physical anguish. Rather than lashing out, in this most intense of moments, he lived his values by requesting forgiveness for his enemies (Luke 23:34).

We suspect we will never become so well differentiated that we could respond as Jesus did in these highly charged settings. Although it may be true that we spend a lifetime pursuing Jesus as a standard and never achieve that standard, it is also true that we can see significant improvement in our ability to be less anxious in the midst of a highly anxious system.

So, where do you begin? Start by learning to see the anxiety in yourself and in the systems around you. "To attain this calmness," Richardson says, "requires us to understand better where, with whom, and in what circumstances, and in what ways we become anxious. Developing greater clarity about our own symptoms of anxiety and how we live them out within the system is critical to being more objective about the larger situation."

Acknowledge the tendency in your hardwiring and the regular encouragement from your culture to blame and diagnose. Master the concepts of differentiation, triangling, and thinking systems. Then begin practicing them.

It takes intentional, consistent effort to change these habits. Learning this new way of thinking is not about learning a set of techniques (though we do indeed offer some techniques in this chapter). Inside-out change is first about *being,* and then about *doing.* Learning this new way of thinking is about the disciplined practice of living out your beliefs and values despite many anxiety-producing obstacles that come your way. In the short run, it requires disciplined internalization of concepts found in this book and others of a similar vein. Then it requires a community of grace and truth (see Chapter Eight) to support long-term efforts at change.

Practices for Calming

With this in mind, we invite you to begin experimenting with a range of ways to focus on your behavior and your part in the living systems in which you participate. Ultimately you must develop and master your own ways to calm yourself. We have found these ideas helpful:

- Increase your self-awareness.
- Monitor your thinking patterns.
- Manage your feelings.
- Slow the pace.

Increase Your Self-Awareness

Most of us are unaware of our anxious reactions. Finding a few safe relationships in which you ask for ongoing feedback about your behavior can help increase your self-awareness. Simply being aware of your anxious tendencies is a great starting place.

In *Reaching Out,* David Johnson introduces "Joharri's window" as a tool for increasing self-awareness. The name comes from its originators, Joe Luft and Harry Ingham. Figure 5.1 expresses how feedback from trusted associates can confirm your view of yourself,

Figure 5.1. Joharri's Window.

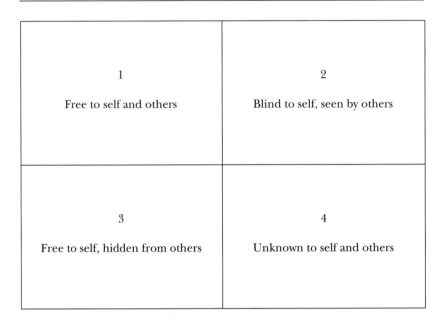

or reveal to you aspects of yourself and consequences of your behavior that you never knew.

"There are certain things you know about yourself and certain things you do not know about yourself. Further, there are certain things that other people know about you and certain things they do not know about you," Johnson writes. The combination of these factors is a framework, a four-part window, through which you can explore means of increasing your self-awareness.

The information in windowpane number one is information that you and others share. You are aware of the information, and those around you have access to the information as well. For instance, people who regularly attend your worship service might know your spouse's name and when you were married.

The information in windowpane number two is information that others see but to which you are blind. For instance, when you become anxious in your relationship with your spouse, you may tend to become quiet and withdrawn in a group. Close friends in your congregation might sometimes describe you as aloof and distant, on the basis of this behavior. However, you have no knowledge whatsoever about how this tendency is experienced by those around you.

The information in windowpane number three is information that is available to you but hidden from others. For instance, you frequently feel irritated when your spouse fails to comment on your sermon during the drive home from church, but you hold those feelings close to yourself and do not share them with anyone else.

The information in windowpane number four is information that is unknown to you and others. The anxiety that arises for you from your spouse's silence on the trip home from church is connected to a pattern in your family of origin. Your father, who rarely voiced criticism, frequently expressed disapproval through silence. You've not yet made that connection, nor has your spouse.

Interaction with others produces new insights. In a visit home over the holidays, your spouse experiences your father's silent treatment. In the long conversation on the drive home, he reflects on his experience with your dad. As he does, internally you make the connection between your experience of your dad and your experience of your spouse when he is silent about your sermon. These insights then move from pane four to pane three. As you disclose them to your spouse, you move them to number one. As you interact with others and get feedback from them, you gain new insights. These insights were in pane two, but through interaction with your friends they move from pane two to pane one. In Johnson's words, "As a relationship grows your free area will become larger and your blind and hidden areas will become smaller. As you become more self-disclosing, you reduce the hidden area. As you encourage others to give you feedback, your blind area is reduced. Through reducing your hidden area you give other people information to react to, thus enabling them to give more informed and precise feedback, which better reduces your blind area. Through reducing your blind area, you increase your self-awareness; this helps you to be even more self-disclosing with others."

A person with few close relationships and little self-awareness might diagram his or her self-awareness as in Figure 5.2.

After developing several close relationships in which appropriate self-disclosure is engaged and feedback received, a person might diagram his or her self-awareness as in Figure 5.3.

Figure 5.2. Low Self-Awareness.

1 Free to self and others	2 Blind to self, seen by others
3 Free to self, hidden from others	4 Unknown to self and others

A leader can increase his or her ability to be less anxious by intentionally using the concepts embodied in Joharri's window to increase self-awareness and thereby gain insight into his or her personal attitudes, feelings, beliefs, and behaviors as they contribute to anxiety in the system.

Monitor Your Thinking Patterns

We all have preferred ways of thinking. Those preferences have been shaped by many influences, among them personal temperament, the functionality of our family of origin, and the stability of the settings in which we live and minister.

Ethan grew up in a chaotic home. His mother, a drug addict and prostitute, was divorced and lived from boyfriend to boyfriend. Ethan was beaten and molested by several of these men. On more than one occasion, his mother was abused and left for dead. It became Ethan's responsibility as a young child to arrange to get his mom to the hospital. Over a lifetime, Ethan developed a pattern of thinking. If he ever

Figure 5.3. High Self-Awareness.

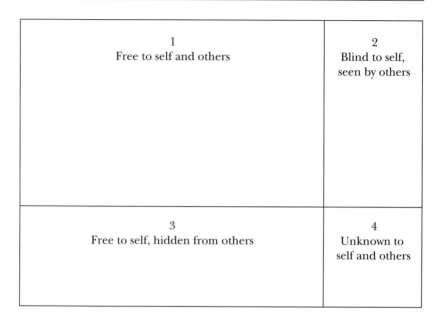

1 Free to self and others	2 Blind to self, seen by others
3 Free to self, hidden from others	4 Unknown to self and others

experienced any chaos in a group setting, he immediately assumed that those in charge were incompetent. He would then engage a series of behaviors designed to take control of the environment.

The survival skills that Ethan learned as a child became a pattern of thinking that was generalized to all situations as an adult. In his life as a pastor, he almost always overfunctioned as a result of his distorted thinking pattern. This is one variety of how distorted ways of thinking lead to increased anxiety.

In *Feeling Good,* David Burns describes common ways of thinking that result from increasing anxiety in a system. Once in place, they also provide feedback that serves to increase the anxiety a person or system experiences:

- All-or-nothing thinking: you see things in black-and-white categories. For example, if your performance falls short of perfect, you're a failure.
- Overgeneralization: you see a single, negative event as a never-ending pattern of defeat.

- Mental filter: you pick out a single negative detail and dwell on it exclusively, so that your vision of all reality becomes darkened, like a drop of ink that discolors a whole beaker of water.
- Disqualifying the positive: you reject positive experiences by insisting that they don't count for some reason or other.
- Jumping to conclusions: you make a negative interpretation even though there are no definite facts that convincingly support your conclusion.
- Mind reading: you make assumptions about someone else's thoughts without bothering to find out what he or she is thinking.
- Fortune telling: you anticipate that things will turn out badly, and you feel convinced that your prediction is a fact.
- Magnification or minimizing: you exaggerate the importance of negative things or inappropriately shrink positive things.
- Emotional reasoning: you assume that your emotions necessarily reflect how things really are ("I feel it, therefore it must be true").
- *Should* statements: you try to motivate yourself with "shoulds" and "shouldn'ts"; the emotional consequence of this is guilt.
- Labeling and mislabeling: instead of describing your error, you attach a negative label to yourself. If someone else rubs you the wrong way, you attach a negative label to him. You use labeling language that is emotionally loaded.
- Personalization: you take things personally. You see yourself as the cause of things that in fact you are not primarily responsible for. You interpret things personally that may have nothing to do with you.

The Apostle Paul calls us to "not be conformed to this world, but be transformed by the renewing of your mind" (Romans 12:2). He goes on to say that this transformation enables us to "prove what is the good, acceptable, and perfect will of God." Leaders who want to become less anxious learn to monitor their thinking patterns. Paul also tells us to "take every thought captive" (2 Corinthians 10:5). When cognitive distortion is a patterned way of thinking, the emotionally mature leader takes responsibility for adjusting those patterns.

Redirecting our thinking is not an easy task. It is like "taping over" a cassette tape. Erasing and replacing messages takes practice and repeated internal correction. Identifying the faulty thinking is a good first step. Sharing your desire to change the behavior with trusted friends helps. Ask them to gently (and perhaps privately) point it out when they see it. Identify a stressful setting in which you are tempted to think in this faulty manner, and then practice the new way of thinking before going into that setting.

Manage Your Feelings

In Ephesians 4, Paul says: "Go ahead and be angry. You do well to be angry—but don't use your anger as fuel for revenge. And don't stay angry. Don't go to bed angry. Don't give the Devil that kind of foothold in your life" (*The Message*).

I (Jim) grew up with the belief that experiencing negative feelings was sin. Rather than learning to manage my feelings so they could fuel a passion for the things of God, I learned to deny and repress them. Somehow I believed that when I experienced anger or fear or sadness, I was sinning. Over a lifetime, I learned to see that Jesus experienced quite a range of emotions. I also learned that he chose when to inject those emotions into the relationship (see Matthew 21:12 as one example).

In my midtwenties, I spent some extended time with a Christian counselor. I was seeking to make sense of the profound low self-esteem that I experienced, and I was looking for tools to help manage my anger. In the early days of our time together, I had a conversation with Joe, my counselor, that went like this:

JIM: Yesterday I was talking to one of the youth workers in our church. He failed to contact a new young person that I had asked him to follow up on.

JOE: How do you feel about his failure to follow up?

JIM: I just can't understand why someone would do that. He said he would do it. He's a responsible adult in every other area of his life. Why does he just blow church off like that?

JOE: That's helpful information. Thanks for sharing it. How do you feel about his failure to follow up?

JIM: He must have had a bad week. I know that his wife's job has her traveling some these days. And with the two small children, I'm sure he has a lot of added assignments.

JOE: That's also helpful information. Thanks for sharing it. How do you feel about his failure to follow up?

JIM: (with considerable exasperation) "I don't know how I feel. You've asked me that three times now, and I'm apparently not giving the right answer."

Joe went on to say, "Let me help you. Basic feelings can be divided into one of four categories. You usually feel mad, sad, glad, or scared."

At first, this seemed artificial to me. Feelings couldn't be that simple. The truth was I had very little experience identifying, talking about, and processing my feelings. I grew up in a culture (family, church, and society) that put a high value on self-sufficiency and a positive attitude. The result of sharing negative feelings was emotional distancing or cutoff—sometimes accompanied by infliction of physical pain. The result was that I learned to repress or deny my feelings.

Over the next few weeks, the same conversation began to go a little differently:

JIM: Yesterday I was talking to one of the youth workers in our church. He failed to contact a new young person that I had asked him to follow up on.

JOE: How do you feel about his failure to follow up?

JIM: Well, let's see . . . mad, sad, glad, or scared. I know it's not glad. I don't think it's mad. So, it's probably sad or scared.

Joe would then help me process these two possibilities, and I would settle in on one of them (or in some cases both). Over time, I did not have to be so conscious of working through what I came to call the "feeling grid." As I began to recognize sadness or anger or fear, the next time it was easier to identify it.

I learned over time that I could (and often did) have feelings of which I was not aware. This became a part of Joharri's windowpane two. Others could see the feelings, and their presence created anxiety for those around me. The fact that I was unaware of them made others doubly anxious. As I learned to understand and explore my feelings, I developed the capacity to process those feelings in a safe place. Then I could decide whether to share them in a relationship or not. I was freer to think clearly because my feelings were not clouding that capacity.

One mistake we often make is blaming others for our feelings, saying something like "Eugene really made me mad." In point of fact, your feelings are a result of your particular wiring, life experience, and perceptions. Eugene engaged in certain behaviors, but your feelings are yours to know and manage. Taking responsibility for one's feelings (not denying them, repressing them, or blaming them on others) is one of the most helpful things a person can do in seeking to be a less-anxious leader.

Leaders who want to become less anxious learn to monitor their feelings. When life experience produces intense feelings, a leader takes responsibility for identifying and processing them appropriately.

The Psalms are full of intense, moving expression of the feelings that anxiety brings to the life of those who hunger after God's presence. Again and again, as the psalmists cry out to God in their anger, fear, or sadness, they find rest in Him. Psalms 6, 23, 27, 31, and 64 are but a few examples.

Slow the Pace

Ted and I (Jim) meet for lunch following a conference where I had presented some concepts from *Leading Congregational Change.* He is encouraged by what he has heard, in part because he is already attempting to practice some of the concepts. He briefly tells me the story of his congregation: a racially diverse, urban congregation with a significant mix of poverty and affluence. Ted has served the congregation for eleven years; he is trusted. He has significant capital in the emotional bank account with a lot of people in the congregation. Nevertheless, he is frustrated with how things are going.

After twenty minutes of conversation, I ask, "When was the last time you had four or more hours of solitude?"

"Well, I'm alone for a number of hours each week as I do sermon preparation."

"I mean solitude in the spiritual-discipline sense of the word. Time where you are quiet before God—not working on any task— just listening and being still."

Ted snorts, "You've got to be kidding! I thought you were the pastor of a church. You must know there's never any time for that."

He goes on to talk about the demands of his life: family, administrative duties, sermon preparation, and pastoral care. He finishes by saying, "I rarely have any time for just me and God. It's all I can do to find the time to connect to him when I've got a task to do."

Ted's candor is both alarming and clarifying. Anxiety intensifies when leaders cannot reflect on their own inner lives and on the life of the system around them. Slowing the pace helps reduce the leader's anxiety.

The first way to slow the pace is by building spiritual disciplines into daily life. The Gospels are full of reminders that Jesus made a practice of setting aside an extended period for prayer and solitude (Luke 4:1–13; Mark 1:35; John 6:15; John 6:22).

How is it that our practice of spiritual discipline works to reduce anxiety? In our anxiety, it is as if we begin to vibrate. Our connection with others means that the anxiety is quickly transferred, and soon the others are vibrating, too. When life begins to shake, the only thing that can calm it is for us to take hold of something solid, something unshakable. Jesus said, "Do not let your hearts be troubled" (John 14:1). The means to quieting a troubled and anxious heart, he said, are to take hold of God in faith: "Trust in God; trust also in me." This is what practicing the spiritual disciplines allows us to do. By trust and obedience we "take hold" of God (more accurately, God takes hold of us), and our troubled hearts begin to calm down. We grow still and know that he is God (Psalm 46:10).

Jesus expresses this dynamic in another form in the Sermon on the Mount, when he tells us to not to "be anxious" about our lives (Matthew 6:25). Instead, we are told to "seek first God's kingdom" (Matthew 6:33), and that it is a kingdom that cannot be shaken (Hebrews 12:28). Paul's directions are similar; in Philippians 4:6 he instructs us to "not be anxious about anything." Instead, we are told to take hold of God by spiritual disciplines such as prayer, supplication, and gratitude. The disciplines work to lower our experience of anxiety. By them, we take hold of a relationship with One who is unshakable, who is so immense that all our vibrating does not disturb him at all. Rather, his peace is transferred to us (John 14:27). Then, as those connected to us find us to be a calm presence, we have an effect on them as well. One who is living in a vital relationship to God, knowing his peace, can have a calming effect on the entire system.

Throughout the ages, the church has found the classic disciplines of the Christian faith to be the resource for keeping believers connected to the life and power of Jesus. Prayer, fasting, solitude, silence, and worship are but a few disciplines that, when engaged, allow the leader to reflect on his or her life. (The spiritual disciplines are discussed more fully in Chapter Eight. Also, see Appendix B for a brief description of some key disciplines.)

In addition to practicing the spiritual disciplines, here are four more suggestions on how to slow the pace.

First, *clarify before responding.* Sometimes anxiety increases because we have misunderstood the message. Recently I (Jim) was talking with a group of pastors. One of them said (about an idea that I thought was a good one), "I think what they are doing is dangerous." Internally, I assumed that because he believed it was dangerous, he also believed that the thing being discussed shouldn't be done. I reacted and began to defend my position. It took several moments of conversation before it became clear that we were actually in agreement. He believed that it was dangerous but worth the risk. I could have reduced the anxiety by simply responding with "Are you saying that this thing shouldn't be done?" He could have completed the communication loop, and my anxiety—as well as his regarding my response—would have been reduced.

Jesus clarified the position of others with questions. "Who do you say that I am?" (Matthew 16:15). "Why do you call me good?" (Mark 10:18).

Second, *breathe and count.* As parents, we learn early on to count to ten before engaging in any act of discipline. The reason is that our anxiety is reduced. Many people, when under stress, literally stop breathing. Some hyperventilate, but most hold their breath unconsciously. A few deep breaths buys us time, delivers oxygen to the brain, and elicits an automatic calming response. A leader can reduce anxiety by simply taking deep breaths and pausing for a moment before responding.

Third, *wait to respond.* When I (Jim) was a child, I would hurriedly run into my parents' room and ask permission to do this or that. My dad would often respond by saying, "If you must have an answer immediately, the answer is no. If I can think about it a while, the answer is maybe." I've learned that his approach was a good one.

Although this can only be inferred from the story of Jesus and the woman in John 8, one can imagine that Jesus was slowing the pace. Perhaps he was thinking through the best response and mastering his emotions while writing in the sand before an angry crowd demanding that she be stoned.

Fourth, *ask for a time-out.* Sometimes a leader needs to intentionally ask for a time-out. The intensity in the room increases so much that, in humility, the leader acknowledges that he or she is not thinking as clearly as might be desired. So the participants agree to return to the conversation another time. For nearly ten years, I (Jim) worked on a team with three people who had an agreement: in any staff discussion, any person on the team had the right to call a time-out. When one of us sensed our anxiety rising, we would take a break to gain some perspective. The result of practicing this discipline was amazing.

Edwin Friedman says (in *A Failure of Nerve*), "The capacity of members of the clergy to contain their own anxiety regarding congregational matters, both those not related to them, as well as those where they become the identified focus, may be the most significant capability in their arsenal. Not only can such capacity enable religious leaders to be more clear-headed about solutions and more adroit in triangles but, because of the systemic effect that a leader's functioning always has on an entire organism, a non-anxious presence will modify anxiety throughout the entire congregation."

Staying the Course

Nathan, to whom you were introduced at the beginning of the chapter, reflects our stories and those of many pastors we know. The church is made up of broken individuals who come with a varying amount of anxiety. As the church lives out the Great Commission, we continuously reach those who have not accessed the resources available through the Holy Spirit to manage their lives well (Matthew 9:12; Luke 19:10). In fact, the more broken are the people we reach, the less likely they are to have the capacity to manage anxiety. In the face of this reality, the demand for highly differentiated leadership that stays connected to those being served is tremendous, and the challenge of providing it is immensely challenging.

Nathan returned to the angry elder who was waiting in the conference room. He listened intently, determined to speak the truth in love (Ephesians 4:15). He reflected the pattern of behavior that he observed in this elder and his family. He calmly declared his personal conviction about conflict and how an effective leader managed conflict. He refused to fix the problem between the two elders. Instead, he urged this elder to take personal responsibility for resolving the conflict by following clear biblical instructions.

In this particular case, the elder and his family left the church. Nathan was both grieved and relieved. Over the next three years, two of the six elders in the church left and went to other churches in the area. After a season of confusion, things began to turn around. Nathan's commitment to focus on his own life—his own anxiety and reactivity—and to increase his capacity to live out his beliefs and values amid a highly anxious congregational system began to pay dividends. It was, and is, a challenging journey, but one that is worth the price.

Self-Assessment Questions

- What are three to five ways you can think of to gain a greater degree of objectivity about the current issues in your congregation or family?
- If you were to describe the situation as objectively as possible, without assigning blame or diagnosing the problem, how would you do it?
- If you were to write down or diagram the situation, reporting only facts and with no interpretation, what would you come up with?
- How would you describe your own role in what is taking place?
- What is your instinctive emotional reaction to the situation? How would you describe the emotions? How would someone on the other side of the issue describe your reaction?

- Under the influence of anxiety, we all find our best thinking distorted. Of the dozen or so distortions (from David Burns) listed earlier, which are your favorites? Do you tend toward some of them more than others? If your spouse or fellow staff member were asked to describe you, which would he or she pick?
- What are three to five ways you can think of to slow the pace of your life as anxiety rises in your congregation or family? Does it feel natural or unnatural to think about doing this at a time that is being defined by others in the system as a crisis?

Part Three

Family Patterns

Chapter Six

Going Home Again

*I will establish my covenant as an everlasting covenant
between me and you and your descendants after you for
the generations to come, to be your God and the God of
your descendants after you.*
—GENESIS 17:7

*When one can understand and alter one's own reactivity
to past generations, there is far more choice in life.*
—VICTORIA HARRISON, IN ROBERTA GILBERT'S
CONNECTING WITH OUR CHILDREN

Antonio came from a long line of evangelists and knew before he
was ten that he would "carry the light" for his generation.

Although no one in the family remembers mentioning it to
Joel, it was his grandmother who looked into his baby face and
said, "This one will make a preacher."

Lisa knew that her parents expected her to choose a profession
that would promise status in the community and a substantial
income. Her decision to go to seminary represented rebellion and
freedom from their expectations.

Lisa, Joel, and Antonio each had his or her own motivation for
becoming a pastor, but they shared one thing: a family system that
shaped the course of their lives.

Too often, we sleepwalk through life, never really knowing
why we do what we do. But as we experience inner transformation through differentiation of self, we redeem and recover our

original calling, separating it from the expectations and influences of family and making it our very own. This kind of differentiation must happen at every level if the self is truly to be reclaimed. We must go home again.

Understanding self in our own family of origin makes it possible to understand who we are in the nuclear family as well as the church family. Because we developed our unique reactive pattern in our family of origin, changing how we relate to that family clears the way for changing our relationships with our spouse, children, and congregation. This means staying connected to the family of origin without being absorbed by it, and remaining less anxious and less reactive in the face of old patterns. We have seen many leaders who find a way to change the patterned reaction they have to their family of origin and are then uniquely empowered to live and minister more freely and more efficiently.

Old Patterns, New Choices

We almost always underestimate the importance of the emotional processes that travel through our extended family into our nuclear family and ultimately into our own lives. This is not to say that our family *causes* us to be the way we are; remember, systems theory is not about blame. Rather, the multigenerational family, as a living organism, transmits anxiety, stress, function, and dysfunction through its ranks. In turn, the individual members of the family learn unique but predictable ways of managing that anxiety. Many of those adaptive responses work against us later as we form intimate relationships with others.

The leader who learns constructive ways of relating to the family of origin solidifies healthy relationships in other areas. By giving attention to the impact that the family of origin has on current functioning, leaders decrease their own anxiety and allow those they lead to do the same.

Forming triangles within the family both creates and relieves anxiety. As each person in the family becomes more or less differentiated, others are set up to follow suit. The generations are the context within which each individual self develops its level of differentiation.

Creating a Family Diagram

A beginning point for understanding our family and our place in it is to create a family diagram. Using symbols for family members and abbreviations for significant information, a family diagram captures several generations of a family on one page. In this way, we can trace the emotional process of the family, noting how our forebears managed chronic anxiety, what triangles formed, and where the places of cutoff are.

A family diagram is not the same as a family tree. True, we are interested in getting down the facts of the family, but not for the sake of genealogy. These facts aid in learning something about the emotional functioning and the level of differentiation of self throughout the generations. A family diagram, according to Kerr and Bowen, simplifies the complex interactions of complicated people and amounts to a kind of shorthand for understanding them. Appendix A has additional information about constructing a family diagram. For now, though, I'd like to share my own (Trisha's) family diagram as an example. I'll begin with my nuclear family (Figure 6.1).

Notice that in a family diagram, males are represented by squares and females by circles.

Figure 6.1. Nuclear-Family Diagram.

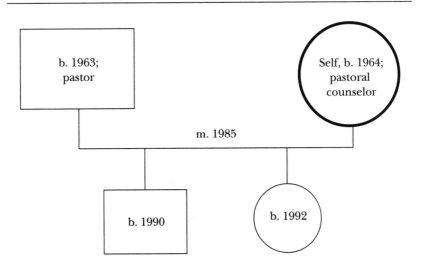

I have included basic information such as the year of birth and marriage and occupation. Adding my immediate family of origin, my family diagram looks like Figure 6.2.

As you can see, this diagram shows three generations: my own, my children's, and my parents'. The adoption of my brothers, the belated birth of my "little sister," and the professions of my parents are each important factors in how my family functioned as well as in my own development. We also begin to detect the presence of symptoms such as clinical depression, which can be traced back through at least three generations. When we diagram one more generation, the picture takes on additional complexity (Figure 6.3).

Now we notice the multigenerational struggle with depression as well as several important places where relationships have been cut off and abandonment has occurred. As I look at this diagram, questions begin to form in my mind:

- What effect did my grandparents' divorce have on my mother? How did that cutoff affect later generations? How did the family use myth to explain the divorce in a time when it carried a stigma?
- What effect did my grandfather's death have on my father? How did my grandmother's life change? How did the family accommodate these changes?
- Notice that, out of ten adults in two generations, six are educators. What are the family values that produce this? What is the effect of those family values on family members?
- What effect did abandonment and adoption have on my brothers? How was our family affected?
- Who is at risk for depression in the third and fourth generations? Is there any way to predict and circumvent that risk?

The Value of the Family Diagram

Although the family diagram does not give us all the answers to our questions, it is useful in several important ways. First, according to Kerr and Bowen, looking at multigenerational emotional process moves the focus away from a specific individual in one's past (particularly off one's inevitably flawed parents) and permits an objective, systemic perspective on one's own family and one's own life. For example, we no longer see ourselves as the victim of our imperfect

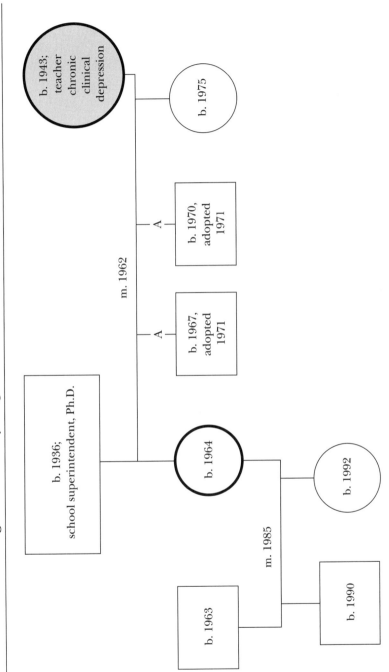

Figure 6.2. Family Diagram with Addition of Family of Origin.

Figure 6.3. Extended Family Diagram.

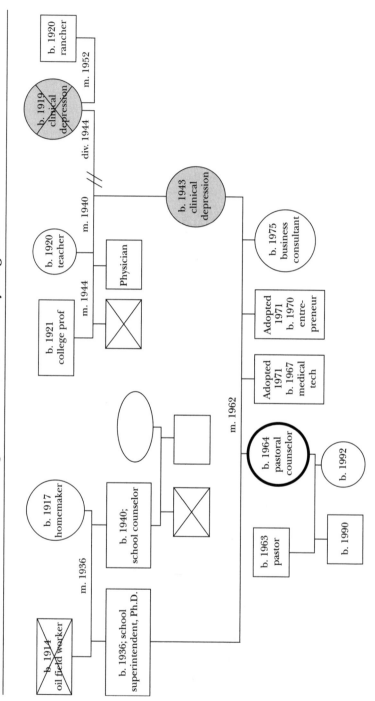

parents. Instead, we see how our parents influenced us, as their parents influenced them, as their parents influenced them, and so on.

Second, the family diagram can highlight possibilities in the future. When I became aware of the current of depression running through my mother's family, I took steps to protect myself from it. In part by educating myself, seeking counseling, and making significant changes in how I thought and managed stress, I have been able to avoid the pattern of depressive thinking and perfectionism that grips the women in my family.

Third, the family diagram focuses solely on facts, helping us see the reality of our emotional upbringing and not old family assumptions about it. All families develop myths. By focusing on the facts, we see what actually happened and not what someone told us happened. Sometimes the process of gathering facts for the family diagram is itself a way for us to connect with family. As the generations are asked to tell their stories, and as buried information is brought to light, family members sometimes begin to excavate old secrets, rediscover family values, and reconnect around shared memories.

Examine Your Sibling Position

Each child grows up in a different family, depending on his or her configuration in that family. The oldest child may have parents who are vigilant and idealistic, while the youngest child in the same family usually has a mother and father who are more relaxed, indulgent, less restrictive, and more tired. Older children may have more of the parents' time and attention, while the family may have more resources available for the younger children.

As we grow up interacting with our brothers and sisters, we learn who we are in relation to other people. We learn to dominate and submit, to placate and compromise, to lead and follow. We learn how to relate to members of the same sex and of the opposite sex. We can even predict how a person learns to react to anxiety by looking at the place in the family that he or she occupies.

Scott, for example, is a youth minister in a large church. He is often complimented for being easy to get along with and good at negotiating. As the fifth of six brothers, learning to get along was not so much a character trait as a survival skill! Learning to be assertive and set clear boundaries does not come so naturally to

Scott, however. Developing these abilities is part of his differentiating process.

Jeremy, on the other hand, serves as pastor in a large church. He is the older brother of one sister. He became dominant in relationships early and still does not always understand when other people do not want to do things his way.

Neither Scott's sibling position nor Jeremy's is better than the other. Because each place in the family constellation has its own set of advantages and disadvantages, no position is preferable to any other. Jeremy must learn to listen and cooperate (strengths Scott has naturally) and Scott must learn to assert himself (which comes easily to Jeremy).

Both Scott and Jeremy can break out of patterned ways of reacting by changing how they relate to their own siblings. For example, when distance and personal problems prohibited his older brothers from planning an anniversary party for their parents, Scott took charge. Although telling his brothers what to do was a new experience, it was a step toward beginning to discard his usual passive stance and be more assertive. Jeremy, on the other hand, found himself changing his view of his "little" sister and began asking her advice about their parents' medical needs. She enjoyed sharing her expertise, and he enjoyed listening and learning for a change.

Changing patterned reactions with siblings is important not only because it may improve those family relationships but because it sets the stage for change in all other significant relationships. After Jeremy learned to be different with his sister, his staff noticed that he was also different with them, less inclined to treat them like little brothers and sisters and more willing to listen to them as valued colleagues. Scott learned to confidently express his opinions to his senior pastor instead of compliantly deferring to him as if he were an older brother.

Bridging Cutoffs

Clearly, returning to family relationships and changing the old ways of behaving open up many new options in a relationship. But what if there is no relationship to which to return? Many families break up into factions of not speaking and not caring. Some family members remain estranged from other family members simply because their parents remain estranged from each other.

According to *Time* magazine (Dec. 18, 2000), up to 10 percent of all American siblings claim to have no relationship with each other. In some families, children grow up and move away and never really reestablish contact with their parents at home. Sometimes the period of being cut off ends when children establish themselves as mature adults and parents mellow and reconcile. Tragically, sometimes the cutoff is forever.

Of course, cutoff can occur even if there is no physical distance. Families may become emotionally fragmented thanks to overwork, isolation, or poor communication. Family members may stay in contact but not be connected. Although they interact with each other to some degree, they shut each other out of their lives and cut themselves off from one another.

When we are cut off from others, we tend to justify our position. "Good riddance," we might say, or, "I don't need that person in my life." However, the person who is emotionally cut off is just as reactive in the relationship as the person who is dependent on others. The level of anxiety in the relationship is just as high and the presence of symptoms just as likely.

The family of Abraham the patriarch experienced the tragedy of cutoff when his son Ishmael was literally banished from his father's house, sent away into the desert, and denied his birthright (Genesis 21:8–21). Many years later, the estrangement was at least partially bridged when Ishmael returned to the family to help Isaac bury their father (Genesis 25:9). We are not told what the two brothers talked about or how they made peace with their family's pain. But in the next generation, another tragic cutoff—this one between Jacob and Esau—also has devastating consequences, and then, as the brothers overcame years of resentment and hatred, a poignant reconciliation occurs (Genesis 33).

In the New Testament, we learn that God has called us to join him in the ministry of reconciliation (2 Corinthians 5:18). Helping others find peace with God and each other is a divinely appointed responsibility. How can we partner with God in bringing harmony to the lives of others when distance and estrangement mark our own family relationships? Failure to face and deal with our own cutoff relationships weakens our capacity to guide others in facing a similar issue. However, if we open ourselves to the possibility of change in our most intimate relationships, we become uniquely qualified to act as a minister of reconciliation with others.

The careful and sometimes painful process of restoring a cut-off relationship is an important way to minimize anxious reactivity and reclaim oneself even in the most difficult relationship. In recent years, I (Trisha) have watched my own mother resist the understandable temptation to cut off the relationship with her mentally ill mother. Instead, she chose to set boundaries. She offered my grandmother loving acceptance without allowing her to control her, and in the end she was able to help her die with dignity in the care of those who loved her.

Changing Patterns in Your Family of Origin

The person seeking transformation, says Roberta Gilbert in *Connecting with Our Children,* faces the challenge of maintaining an emotional connection with each generation of the family while learning to disengage from some of the family's anxious patterns. By learning to define ourselves in our family, we increase our ability to define ourselves in our other relationships. This is why we must go home again.

Establish Connections

The first step toward going home again as a more differentiated self is the commitment to stay in touch with the extended family without being absorbed by the considerable anxiety attached to those relationships. If anxiety compels us to distance ourselves from certain people, differentiation requires that we connect with those same people. Since connecting with people who do not create anxiety in our lives does little to move us up the scale of differentiation of self, the relationships we run from may be the very ones we should run toward. When we find that we have sacrificed self to a particular relationship, recovering that self in the context of the original relationship is vital.

There are no rules for making contact with extended family. If cutoff has been particularly acrimonious, a letter preceding a telephone call or visit may give the other person time to respond to the overture rather than reacting. If the relationship has been ongoing but superficial and distant, the person pursuing change has to use creativity and a new way of relating.

Willing to risk rejection, Kevin asked his father, a motorcycle enthusiast, to ride across the state with him to a conference. At truck stops and motels, Kevin listened to his father talk about motorcycle trivia, his recent marriage, and his childhood. By resisting the temptation to impose his own expectations and agenda on the weekend, Kevin was able to "just be" with his father and enjoy a new level of connection they had never enjoyed in the past.

Work on Each Relationship Individually

Although I (Trisha) am close to both my parents, I tended to relate to my sister, Christy, through my mother and to my brothers through my dad. I would ask about my siblings, find out what was going on in their lives, and delude myself into thinking I had real relationships with them. Recently, my mother subtly stepped back from the triangle I had formed with my sister and her. Since she would no longer carry information back and forth, I began to deal with Christy directly. We exchanged e-mail and spoke by telephone more often. Last summer, for the first time, my children and I spent several days at her house. I realized that although I loved my sister, I had become lazy, relying on my mother to do the work of keeping us connected. Wisely, my mother defined herself in relation to her two daughters—as an encouraging friend but not as a go-between.

Many families allow one person to form the hub of all familial relationships. Leslie said, "If I call my parents and my dad answers the phone, I don't know what to do. I love my dad, but he doesn't talk. I talk to my mother and then she tells my father what he needs to know. I don't think I've ever really had a conversation with my dad." She must learn to engage her father in conversation and form a relationship with him individually.

Leslie could pursue a relationship with her father in a variety of ways. Asking about his childhood and his younger years allows her to hear more about the shaping events in his life and gives her more information about her family system. Sharing her anxiety about a problem gives her father the chance to be helpful by drawing on his own experience. For fourteen years, I (Trisha) had not heard my grandmother talk about her deceased oldest son until I talked openly about my fears about delivering my first child. She was able to reassure me, and we connected our relationship to the memory of a valued member of the family.

Working on oneself in a relationship with a family member is even possible after the person has died, or cannot be contacted, or is otherwise inaccessible. The relationship can still be pursued by proxy. Lori's mother died when she was nine, and Lori had only shadowy memories of her. Her father abruptly relocated his motherless daughters, remarried, and discouraged any contact between them and his new wife's family. Battling severe depression, Lori realized that she needed to understand herself better as the daughter of her mother and as a young woman about to become a mother herself. She contacted her mother's sisters and arranged a week-long reunion. Amid tears and laughter, Lori heard the stories of her mother's life and death and her own childhood for the first time. In the context of a renewed relationship, Lori began to see herself as a grown woman and not just as a motherless child.

Give Up on Changing the Family

To be truthful, most people are less interested in focusing on their own challenges in being a self and are more interested in changing the others in their family. Understanding family interactions becomes just one more set of tools to be used in the effort to exchange the family they have for the family they want. The problem is, families resist even the best efforts of their members to force change, and as the family polarizes, change becomes even less likely.

The phrase "I'm going to confront my family about . . ." is a sure sign that the focus is on changing the family and not on differentiating self. Another tip-off is the question "How can I get my family to . . . ?" Overfocusing on the failings of the family—and there are usually plenty—is another way we keep the spotlight on our desire for our family to change rather than on our ability to change within our family. However much we might want them to, family members almost never change by being confronted, manipulated, or blamed.

Even as we say "I know I can only change myself," many of us harbor the slightly irrational belief that if we can only say the right things or do the right things, the people in our families will change for the better. This may occur, but it cannot be the driving energy for our efforts. We have many options as we seek to keep the focus where it belongs, which is on ourselves:

- We accept the challenge of changing self as we relate to our family, without taking on the impossible task of trying to change the family.
- We let our own thinking be known in the family without trying to force the family to adopt it.
- We pay attention to our own past contributions to our family's situation as well as to our own current choices.
- We avoid relating to the family as priest or therapist, but only as self.
- We accept that this is the family we have instead of struggling against this reality.

These are perhaps the most difficult aspects of differentiation of self to maintain.

Prepare for the Family's Response

People consistently undermine their own efforts at differentiation of self by failing to anticipate the family's reaction to them and plan their own response. After the first well-rehearsed moments of contact are over, the good intentions dissolve and the old patterns of acting and reacting resume. Someone says, "But my family knows how to push all my buttons," and this is undoubtedly true. This is why it is necessary to strategize and plan for a new way to respond when those buttons get pushed!

Once a family's anxiety has been heightened by change in a member, it typically offers one of three responses: (1) "You're wrong," (2) "Change back," or (3) "If you don't, these are the consequences" (also known as "Or else"). These responses may be expressed in many ways, but they are extremely predictable. If we do not anticipate and prepare for them, our efforts at differentiation will fail. We are likely to return, Peter Titelman suggests, with a sense of defeat to the family's normal way of doing things, or fight back, or withdraw, or run away.

Most people know their own family members well enough to anticipate how they will react to their effort at differentiation. For example, if the silent treatment is a common change-back response in my family, I must plan a new way to manage my anxiety when it happens. I can plan to breathe deeply, strategize how to resist the pressure to give in to the family anxiety to restore peace, and decide beforehand how I will respond when no one is talking to me. I can also:

- Remember that other family members may feel their own positions are being threatened by the changes I am making.
- Say what I have chosen to say. It may need to be repeated. I can resist being drawn off course by other issues.
- Anticipate all the ways the family might express its "you're-wrong" and "change-back" messages; I can assemble strategies for continuing to define myself in the face of their resistance.
- Predict the likely consequences for my continued differentiation of self, and decide beforehand that I can tolerate the "or-else" response.

Does this mean that every family will always respond negatively to the positive changes a member makes? Well, yes and no. The initial reaction, grounded in anxiety, is almost always unsupportive. However, the person who anticipates this and perseveres may then find that other family members are also able to begin functioning at a higher level and the interactions within the family may change for the better.

Stand Apart from the Emotional Process of the Family

For most of us, trying to follow the emotional interactions of our family while we are with them is like trying to follow the plot of a movie while sitting too close to the screen.

Without a little healthy distance, we are unable to separate overwhelming feelings and images from the reality of the situation. The objective help of a counselor or coach can be priceless as we struggle for this realistic perspective. Learning to systematically ask and answer a few meaningful questions gives us the objectivity that we seek:

- What is really going on here?
- What am I feeling? What is going on inside me?
- Where is the anxiety in this situation?
- Where are the triangles?
- What choices do I have?

The answers to the questions are important, but equally important is the process of asking them. By paying attention to what is going on around us as well as to the emotional processes within us, we are able to make better choices about our responses. We are less likely, then, to react irrationally and more likely to respond according to our principles. Paying attention to our feelings gives us the data we need to manage them, making it less likely that they will overpower us.

After examining his family history, Austin (first mentioned in Chapter One) realized that his tendency to scream and grab and shake his wife when he was angry was a patterned response learned from his father. With his wife's help, he began to notice how much his parents still shout at each other and speak to each other rudely and disrespectfully. During an extended holiday stay, Austin focused on managing his own feelings of anxiety without participating in the familiar hostility. As the decibel level went up, he focused on his own voice and made choices about how he wanted to communicate with his mother and father. Instead of retreating into familiar behavior like shouting or sarcasm, he chose to listen more. When listening became too difficult, he explained that he needed to calm down and then left the room.

Although Austin's parents never changed their behavior and continued to loudly insult each other, he returned home from his visit with more awareness and less stress than he had ever experienced after a trip home. He felt better about himself and more confident in his ability to change how he handled his own anger.

Prayer is a good way to address these questions in a dialogue with God. Rather than running away from the family, we bring it and ourselves into dialogue with Another. Through prayer, I (Trisha) am often reminded to avoid the childish narcissism of thinking everything that happens in my family is personal—that is, about *me*. I am then freed to respond with the wisdom of an adult rather than the self-centeredness of a child. I often pray for the ability to see things in my family as they really are, not as they seem to be or as I believe they should be. This kind of prayer reminds me to stand apart from the emotional process of my family, participating in it but not overwhelmed by it.

The long journey toward differentiation transforms the soul and ultimately shapes the future. It is a journey toward understanding ourselves in our own context—the generations that shaped us and continue to influence us. First, however, the path of inner change leads us not forward but back—through the generations, back to the original family, back home.

Self-Assessment Questions

- How would you relate your sense of call into ministry to your nuclear or extended family?
- What is your place in the constellation of the family of origin: oldest, youngest, middle? Were you a brother with younger sisters? Younger brothers? Older sisters? Older brothers? How did the unique spot in the family that you occupied help shape you in learning to relate to the same and the opposite sex?
- How would you draw your own family diagram? Try to go back at least three generations (to your grandparents). Talk to people in the family to gather as many details and stories as possible. What do you really know about these people? Where do you find expressions of cutoff in your family? Where has there been conflict? Where have symptoms occurred? Become as curious about this family as you can. Ask lots of questions. Make them your own personal research project.
- If you were to make it a goal to establish a personal, one-to-one relationship with every living member of this family, where would you start? Why? Which ones would be the most difficult to engage?
- If either of your parents is deceased, how would you go about reengaging that relationship? Where could you go to find the information about the dead parent that you would need if you are to understand him or her more fully as a person?
- As you think about this family, where do you find yourself most tempted to place blame, to diagnose, or to practice cause-and-effect thinking?
- If you attempted to engage your family in an effort to differentiate, what issue would arise? How would you think about going among them and being different than you usually are? What would their likely reaction be? How would you think about responding to the reaction differently? In which relationship would change be most difficult for you to sustain?

Chapter Seven

The Nuclear Family

At new, higher levels of personal differentiation, the ability to see process as it unfolds, as well as one's own part in that process, makes it less likely for the relationship to get stuck in patterns and issues. At higher levels of differentiation, relationships serve whatever togetherness needs there may be, but since there are fewer togetherness needs, the two tend to function as a more harmonious team. Individuality is never lost in high level relationships. Rather, in and throughout all the teamwork, there exist two total and complete individuals, fully aware of self and the other, in open communication with each other. That is the ideal.
—ROBERTA GILBERT, *EXTRAORDINARY RELATIONSHIPS*

For this reason, a man will leave his father and mother and be united to his wife, and they will become one flesh.
—GENESIS 2:24

After fifteen years of marriage and thirteen years of ministry, Eddie and Sheryl were getting a divorce. Neither seemed to understand how things had deteriorated to this point, but each saw it as the other's fault. Eddie was particularly angry. "All I wanted was a wife to love me, take care of our family, and help me in ministry," he said. "Instead, I got a woman who is critical, depressed, and frigid." He practically hissed his last accusation.

Sheryl turned to him in fury. "You're right—I don't want to have sex with you when you demand it and manipulate me for it. I'm sick and tired of taking care of you—taking care of your ego, your ministry, your needs. When we were dating, I thought you were so confident, so self-assured. I didn't know that you just thought the world revolved around you and that you expected me to, as well." Sheryl dissolved in angry tears. Eddie rolled his eyes and walked across the room to look out the window.

Of course, most clergy marriages do not end in divorce. But there is no evidence that ministers and their spouses are any better at having a healthy, intimate marriage than is the public at large. In fact, a survey conducted by the Fuller Institute of Church Growth determined that:

- Eighty percent of pastors believed that pastoral ministry affected their family negatively
- Thirty-three percent said ministry was an outright hazard to their family
- Thirty-seven percent confessed having been involved in sexually inappropriate behavior with someone in the church

Like all others, clergy couples struggle with finding time to spend together, financial difficulties, poor communication, and sexual problems (so find H. London and Neil Wiseman in *Pastors at Risk*). Rearing children in today's world is as difficult as it has ever been, and a pastor's family is not exempt from those pressures, either. Many ministry families are anxious, conflicted, and confused.

In this book, we have described a different way of thinking about the world and our place in it. We have looked at the importance of thinking about the role of leadership in a living system and differentiation of self. We have applied these concepts and others to help us engage the personal transformation that is needed if we are to offer effective spiritual leadership in today's environment. In the quest for maturity, the nuclear family is the final frontier. As many of us have discovered, the well-differentiated life is most difficult to live with our spouse and children, even though we sincerely desire to be our best selves with the people we love most. We now turn our attention to the possibilities for learning to do the right thing in our nuclear family.

Do Two Halves Really Make a Whole?

My (Trisha's) daughter Rebecca received a necklace as a prize at a birthday party. The pendant separates into two pieces, each on its own piece of string. Broken apart, the pieces are jagged and incomplete. However, if placed side by side, they fit together to form an intact heart, emblazoned with the word *LOVE*. Rebecca's necklace is the perfect representation of the romantic ideal that forms the foundation for courtship, marriage, and family in Western culture.

This is the notion of love depicted in the movie *Jerry Maguire*, starring Tom Cruise and Renee Zellweger. In the film, Jerry is a self-absorbed but vulnerable man pursuing a woman who realizes that he does not truly love her. However, at the end of the movie, he finally tells her what she has longed to hear: "You complete me." In 1996, when the movie was a hit, romantics everywhere quoted that line to describe what they yearned for in their relationship.

There is only one problem with this idea of love and devotion: over time, it is likely not to work so well. Mathematics aside, intimate relationships are the one place where one half plus one half do not—and never will—make a whole. In the highest-functioning marriage, two mature and complete people unite under God to form an even greater whole, a relationship that transcends the sum of the parts.

More often, though, we look for a partner who will, we hope, complete the unfinished or immature part of ourselves. A man who has difficulty expressing his emotions is likely to seek out a woman who leads with her heart. A young woman, unsure of herself and her worth, will be attracted to a man who seems to have all the answers and promises to take care of her. In the short run, both get what they were looking for: someone to make them feel intact and fulfilled.

The relationship may work out well for a time. However, by relying on the other for the "missing part" of the self, people often cheat themselves and each other of the opportunity to grow in their area of weakness. Worse, they often begin to resent the very qualities in the other that were initially so appealing. The man who is attracted to the more emotional woman may eventually scorn her for being weak or irrational. The woman who seeks out a self-confident partner may begin to resent him for being dominating and controlling. Movies don't go on to show this part of the story.

A pastor, as much as anyone, is certainly vulnerable to this tendency to choose a spouse on the basis of self-completion. For example, a male pastor may be under pressure to find a woman who will be a "good minister's wife" as defined by his church or denomination. Women sometimes marry men who plan to go into the ministry as a way of securing their own status in the church.

During my seminary days, I (Trisha) noticed how often the men in my classes referred to their wives only in reference to themselves. "She's the perfect pastor's wife," one might say. "Her gifts complement my ministry perfectly. I don't think I could do my ministry without her." Although the man would intend his comments to be positive, he was unaware of how he spoke of his wife only in terms of how she related to him. I was always delighted when I heard a man talk about his wife in her own right, with a unique set of gifts and interests all her own.

The tendency to choose someone who compensates for my own deficiencies creates a marriage based on the prospect that this person will meet my needs and fulfill my expectations. The idea that my spouse and I will be two separate people with differing needs and sometimes with competing expectations is rarely part of the contract. Power struggles soon ensue over whose needs are going to be met and at whose expense.

Forces of Togetherness and Individuality in Marriage

As we discussed earlier, two forces are at work in every intimate relationship, whether we are aware of them or not. One is the *togetherness force*, encompassing all our needs for attachment and approval. This force drives us to give up our own beliefs for the sake of stability in the relationship. The other is the *individuality force*, which drives us to seek out independence and autonomy. It impels us to clarify and live out our unique mix of beliefs, gifts, and passions. However, we do not live in an ideal world. We are always vulnerable to excesses, and in the nuclear family we are especially vulnerable to the togetherness force.

In recent years, the Christian church in America has organized itself around the family unit, emphasizing the importance of family relationships, especially those between husband and wife and parents and young children. This has been a largely positive move, correcting the tendency of the larger culture to devalue the family. However, Jesus made it clear that his disciples would face the difficult challenge of defining themselves even in the context of their family. "Do not suppose that I have come to bring peace," he told them, reminding them that their choice to follow him would cost them their dearest relationships (Matthew 10:34–39).

As we have seen, even Jesus chose to do the right thing in the face of opposition from his mother and brothers. He constantly defined himself in terms of his mission and his values while others tried to define him in terms of his family relationships (Matthew 13:55; Luke 11:27; Mark 3:31–35). When his brothers—whether skeptical or concerned for his safety—tried to pressure him to deviate from his chosen path, he briefly explained his position and then did the right thing (John 7:1–10). Jesus was concerned about his family's well-being to the end, taking steps to care for his mother even from the cross. But we never see him bowing to the pressure of his family or altering his values in an effort to please them. We also never see him using his authority to forcibly change their mind about who he was. In Jesus' life, the togetherness forces and the individuality forces operated in a balanced, meaningful way.

The togetherness forces lead people to seek out a relationship, fall in love, get married, and raise a family. But these same forces also fire up emotional intensity between family members to the point that the relationship's survival requires each partner to unwillingly give up individual thoughts and feelings. Roberta Gilbert says that when anxiety in the relationship is high and the emotional maturity of the spouses is low, the togetherness forces lead the partners to abandon the quest to develop a whole, separate self and to attempt instead to complete a self through relationship with the other person.

When I (Jim) married Betty, I brought to the relationship a fairy-tale image of what marriage should be. In my mind, Betty was the person who would meet every unmet need in my life. The weight of that expectation was too heavy to bear. I will never forget the night she said to me, "I need some space. You are smothering me." Those words wounded me, and I thought our marriage was over. Because my own parents never expressed their conflict openly in the presence of their children, I had no context to understand that two adults who loved one another might not always want to be together. Betty held her ground while continuing to reassure me of her love. Over time, we formed relationships with other couples, and I formed friendships with other men, that helped satisfy some of my needs. Balancing the togetherness force with the individuality force brought a new level of intimacy to our marriage.

Roberta Gilbert describes how a couple driven to extremes by togetherness forces might react. They might become embroiled in constant conflict. They might be distantly polite, "allergic to closeness," or overly involved in each other's lives. One partner might dominate the other, who, in turn, loses self in an effort to submit to the other. Or both spouses might focus on one or more children rather than dealing openly with the anxiety in the marriage. In any case, a relationship marked by this kind of fusion is characterized by polarization, emotionally based decision making, and taking sides. Gilbert suggests that each tries to get the other to change; each is preoccupied with the other's deficiencies, and each resolutely refuses to focus on the self.

In contrast, when a couple learns to focus not only on their drive toward togetherness but also on their mutual need for individuality, they are free to be two whole people. This increases the likelihood of their becoming partners united by loyalty, commitment, and common purpose rather than two incomplete people dependent on each other for their emotional survival. Surely this is what it means to be "one flesh" in the richest sense. Such a couple is able to move freely between intimacy and autonomy. They refrain from imposing their expectations on each other but define themselves according to their beliefs, keeping the focus on their own lives and choices while communicating openly and clearly with each other.

When confronted with these ideas, Eddie and Sheryl eventually decided not to divorce. Eddie spent more than a year working with a Christian psychotherapist, seeking to understand his almost compulsive need to enlist others (especially Sheryl) in building up his ego and making himself feel important. He looked at how he manipulated Sheryl (as well as his congregation) to do things his way or to give in to his opinions. He gradually stopped seeing his wife's commitment to her own differing opinions as betrayal or disloyalty.

Sheryl was suspicious of Eddie's efforts for most of that year. However, she accepted the help of the same Christian counselor in dealing with her chronic feelings of depression. Slowly, she learned to focus on her own tendency to overvalue taking care of the needs of others and undervalue taking care of herself. When she learned to communicate clearly with Eddie about her feelings and needs, she was less likely to resort to more passive ways of expressing herself, such as criticizing him or withholding sex. Eventually, Eddie and Sheryl began to work together on their marriage, finding a way to stay connected with each other while focusing on becoming their own best selves.

Thinking Systems in the Nuclear Family

When couples and families seek counseling with me (Trisha) for their relationship difficulties, I have noticed that they are almost never ready to think about their situation in terms of the family's interaction as a whole. Instead, family members want to tell me who in the family is the "cause" of the family's problem and enlist my support in blaming and then changing that person. When I explain that I am neither judge nor referee and that the situation is probably more complicated than they realize, they often look crestfallen and confused.

Their disappointment is understandable. Most of us automatically think in terms of cause and effect. When we see an effect in our relationships, such as conflict or depression, we immediately look for the cause. Our thinking appears logical on the surface: if I can decide who is responsible for my problem, I can change that person and then my problem will be solved. In our struggle to understand our relationships, we tend to focus on how other people treat us. This kind of cause-and-effect thinking pushes us to consider people in our lives only in terms of how they relate to us. We become the center of our own universe. Unfortunately, things are almost never that simple.

As we have seen in previous chapters, thinking systems means remembering the big picture: each member of the family is part of a series of increasingly larger systems (the extended family, the church, the culture, and so on) that have an impact on us and are in turn affected by us. Therefore, a problem with any one member of a family is usually a bigger problem, touching the system as a whole. The good news is that it takes only one family member to make a positive change (in how he or she relates to the family) to change the whole family. When the family changes, every other family member has new opportunities to make changes of their own.

In fact, when we learn to see ourselves as part of a larger, living system (the family), we break free from the self-centeredness that cause-and-effect thinking induces. We now realize that we are part of a meaningful whole, neither more nor less important than the other parts. Rather than demanding that the system revolve around us and our needs and preferences, we are able to follow Paul's admonition to "look not only to your own interests but also to the interests of others" (Philippians 2:4), realizing that they too are valuable parts of the whole.

In her writing on family, Gilbert demonstrates the importance of thinking systems in family functioning:

> If parents think systems, they can learn to recognize all the difficulties out there, the ones within the self and the ones in their families, and know the difference. They can see the system as well as any individual in it, with its problems and their own. They can see their personal strengths and those in their families and begin to operate from that perspective. They can become more sure of their guiding principles and constantly make the daily effort it takes to live within them. They can define their principles to themselves and their children and know that, even when it seems they are not, they are making a difference.

By thinking systems, we lay the groundwork for the intentional changes that transform our family.

Anxiety in the Family System

Many of the problems and difficulties that a family experiences are the result of chronic anxiety in the family system. Anxiety leads to more anxiety, and more anxiety leads to reactivity—an automatic, emotion-driven response. Rather than calmly thinking through possibilities, members of the family react, as Harriet Lerner says in *The Dance of Intimacy,* "reflexively doing what [they] always do, which only leads to more of the same." Anxious reactivity results in rigid relationship patterns that become increasingly intense.

This patterned behavior then undermines the well-being of the family. Gilbert reminds us, in *Connecting with Our Children,* of the five most common reactive patterns: "Under the effects of anxiety, emotionally based patterns of relationship behavior intensify. People do more of what they have always done; it would take a lot of thought to do anything differently. That is, they fight (engage in conflict), flee (distance themselves), cut off entirely, overfunction/underfunction (dominate each other or subordinate to the other), or they focus their anxiety on a child (triangle). These postures, while mitigating anxiety for the short term, will add to it over the long haul" (Gilbert, 1998, p. 75.)

Philip and Elise considered themselves to have a happy marriage. After nine years of marriage and two children, they finished college and seminary and moved to a large city where Philip began his first pastorate. They pointed with satisfaction to the fact that they almost never quarreled and never raised their voices in anger. But when Philip confessed to Elise that he was habitually and compulsively viewing pornography on his church office computer, they were motivated to look more carefully at the patterns of anxiety and reactivity in their marriage.

What they learned surprised them both. First, Philip realized that he was most vulnerable to the temptations of pornography when he felt unappreciated and overwhelmed, which, as the young pastor of a conflict-ridden church, he often did. After a negative meeting with a church member, he would frequently withdraw to his office to lick his wounds. One day, in an effort to distract himself from the mounting anxiety he felt, Philip decided to surf the Web. Before he knew it, he was searching out pornographic Websites. As the excitement of risk and arousal increased, Philip's awareness of his anxiety decreased. He felt powerful and energized. He was hooked.

Later, as he reflected on that day, Philip remembered being ten years old, sneaking his father's *Playboy* magazines to his bedroom, and looking at them when his parents' fighting became intense. Although he had not been tempted by pornography through most of his teenage and young adult years, he now found himself irresistibly drawn to it. Although Philip had escaped the pressures of his parents' conflictual marriage and resisted duplicating that in his own marriage, he was completely unaware of his tendency to withdraw physically and emotionally when anxiety threatened.

Elise also tended to distance herself when she was anxious. Early in their marriage, she kept her feelings of loneliness and her frustration with Philip's emotional unavailability to herself, as her mother had taught her a good Christian wife should. When their two sons were born, Elise focused her attention on them. Soon, both children were sleeping in the couple's king-size bed because they were afraid to sleep in their own rooms.

Fortunately, Philip and Elise were quick to see their problems in terms of the larger family system. Rather than blaming each other, they noticed the relational patterns that had developed and worked hard to change them. Philip began to pay attention to his own emotional well-being. He realized that when he exercised or went fishing with a friend, the temptation to lock himself in his office with his computer waned. He put a stop to his tendency to give all his time and energy to the most negative aspects of church life, bringing the leftovers home to Elise and the children, with nothing left for himself. Instead, he forced himself to leave the office every evening and eat dinner with his family. When he encountered conflict at the church, he picked up the phone and talked to Elise. When the temptation to turn on the computer became intense, he left the office and walked in the woods behind the church, praying the Psalms (particularly Psalm 51, which he memorized). Breathing deeply and walking briskly, he regained his perspective on conflict and learned to tolerate the anxiety until it passed.

For her part, Elise began to share the loneliness she felt in the marriage when Philip withdrew from her. He taught himself not to hear this as criticism but as helpful feedback and trusted her when she said she felt he was moving away from her. When that happened, he was careful to renew his attempts to stay emotionally connected to her. She remained a devoted mother, but she refocused her attention on having fun with Philip, no longer demanding that they take the boys every time they went out at night. As that triangle was minimized, Philip and Elise began to work together to set limits for the children regarding their bedtime routine. Soon both boys were sleeping through the night in their own beds. By dealing with their anxiety in new ways, Philip and Elise actually minimized the anxiety in their lives.

Of course, not all anxiety is problematic. When a threat is real, the resulting anxiety helps us take protective action. A certain amount of anxiety challenges us to try new things and keeps us creative. However, because chronic anxiety adds stress to an already stressed family system, changes the emotional climate of the family, and polarizes family members, it is important to learn to understand it and respond to it thoughtfully. The process by which we learn to do this is called *differentiation*.

Differentiation of Self in the Nuclear Family

Without a commitment to personal change, differentiation is impossible. Unfortunately, we want our lives to change but we resist changing ourselves. Instead, we continue to intensely pursue rigid relationship patterns and then expect others to change in response. Of course, that never works.

We know a psychologist who tells clients who are resistant to a suggestion, "I don't want you to change at all; just do this one thing a little differently." That usually helps her client make a small, manageable change without a great deal of anxiety. However, if we want to pursue a transformed life, we must be willing to make changes in ourselves and how we relate to others. The suggestions given here may help you think about making changes as you relate to your family.

Focus on the Connection

While we were writing this book, on September 11, 2001, about three thousand people lost their lives in a terrorist attack on the United States. From cell phones and computers and even pagers, people facing inevitable death took the opportunity to connect with their families one last time. One man trapped in his office sent a final message to his family: "Fire here. Love you." Another man asked the airline operator to say the Lord's Prayer with him and give his love to his family before his plane crashed into a field in Pennsylvania. People on another doomed flight shared their cell phones, calling home, giving final instructions, and saying "I love you."

Americans were reminded that nothing in our lives matters more than the people. For days, people were asking themselves and each other, "Who would you have called?" According to a *Time*/CNN poll published in the magazine on November 19, 2001, 62 percent experienced a need to spend more time with family members, and 66 percent were moved to tell family members that they loved them. Many took steps to reconcile relationships that were broken or strained. At least for a while, the divorce rate declined. Relationships became more precious than making money, more valuable than meeting a deadline, more important than finishing a list of things to do.

As Christians, we were supposed to know that already. Jesus said that the only thing more important than our love for the people in our lives is our love for God (Matthew 22:37–40). He placed relationships at the center of the spiritual universe. Unfortunately, daily life works against forming and nurturing deep, loving relationships. We become so busy doing tasks that we have no time to be with people. A minister becomes so overwhelmed with projects that someone's personal need can feel like an annoying interruption. As we become busier, we become less open to the inconveniently serendipitous nature of relationships. As our hearts close up, our family suffers.

We must especially learn to stay connected to people in our family when it is hardest to do so. The natural response to a difficult relationship is to pull back, push away, and distance ourselves. When a teenager does not follow the house rules, we lecture more and listen less. When a spouse is thoughtless or inconsiderate, we pout and sigh. When a family member fails to meet our expectations, we withdraw emotionally to avoid disappointment. In contrast to these natural reactions is the father in Jesus' story of the prodigal son, who kept his relationship with his son alive even when the son was literally and emotionally far away (Luke 15:20–24). Even if negative emotions are intense, we can work hard to keep a strong connection with our loved ones while we work out our problems.

A necessary ingredient of a connected relationship is time— quality time and quantity time, and both in abundance. The notion of quality time being enough for our family is a myth. We should make every effort to make our time with our spouses and children high-quality, but nothing can make up for the importance of just being present. Reflecting on his life in his memoir *Just As I Am,*

Billy Graham wrote, "I have many regrets . . . I would do many things differently. For one thing, I would speak less and study more, and I would spend more time with my family. . . . Every day I was absent from my family is gone forever."

My (Trisha's) husband will not have such regrets. Like most pastors, he has an overwhelming schedule and is genuinely committed to doing a good job. One day, though, he came home, looked me in the eye, and said, "I don't know how, but things are going to change. I realized something today. There are a lot of people who can do the things I'm doing. But I'm the only one who can be your husband, and I'm the only one who can be Andrew's and Rebecca's daddy. I am going to be who I need to be for my family." With gratitude, I can say that Craig has followed through on that commitment and it has made all the difference in the world.

Learn to Define Self

All of us long to have a place where we can be ourselves. We want a safe haven where we can be who we really are without the pressure to be who others want or expect us to be. Ministers and their families especially long for a port in a storm of needy people and unrealistic expectations. We long for our home to be such a place of safety. We are often disappointed.

We underestimate the courage it takes to differentiate a self at home, where the love and approval of the people we care about most is at stake. However, until we learn to do so, we have no hope of creating the kind of home we long for. Differentiation of self at home means courageously talking about what we truly think and feel. It means choosing to be who we are with each other rather than living out of an image or a persona. We clearly communicate our limits with each other, defining what is acceptable to us in a relationship out of our best thinking, and what is not. We allow our partners and children, Harriet Lerner says, to do the same.

Unfortunately, we tend to do just the opposite. There are two ways we fail to be a self at home, and most of us tend toward one extreme or the other. On one end of the continuum are those who sacrifice self in an effort to preserve the perceived harmony of the relationship. These folks buy an uneasy peace by their silence or their efforts at conformity. They do not say what they think, they give in too easily when conflict arises, and they discount their own feelings and beliefs.

At the other end of the continuum are those who require the compliance of others to feel secure in the relationship. These people view disagreement as disloyalty, get angry when others express a divergent view, and persistently argue to persuade others to change their mind. Both styles, though highly contrasting, have the same goal in mind: preserving the relationship in the face of anxiety. However, by polarizing in this way, they guarantee the loss of intimacy.

Jerry was a pastor who led his church by the force of his personality. Opinionated and persuasive, he clearly outlined the directions the church should go in, and the positions the church should take; for the most part, the people followed. Not surprisingly, Jerry's wife, Doris, decided early in their marriage to take the path of least resistance. By the time I (Trisha) met them, they had been living at opposite ends of the spectrum for thirty years. Jerry had become a bully, Doris had become a doormat, and neither of them was happy.

In her effort not to sacrifice her own identity (as her mother had done), their daughter Kristen developed a relationship style similar to her father's but with one very interesting twist: what he thought was black, she said was white. Whereas he was an avowed Republican, she campaigned for every Democrat who ran for county office. Jerry loved to barbecue; Kristen was a vegetarian. Every night at supper there was a battle. Kristen would state her opinion about something and Jerry would begin, nicely at first, to argue her out of her position. As he did so, he would become more and more upset and Kristen would become more and more attached to her position. Most evenings ended with doors slamming and angry accusations: "No daughter of mine is going to think that!" and "You can't change me! I'm entitled to my opinion!"

Eventually, Jerry told Kristen that if she voted for the Democratic candidate for president, she would have to move out of the house. She left before election day.

I do not know if Jerry and Kristen ever reconciled. When I last saw them, they were both angry and bitter. For her part, Doris clenched her teeth and kept her mouth shut. I never knew what she really thought about the tension between her husband and her daughter.

I cared about this family. They were each committed believers, involved in loving, meaningful ministries. What if each of them had found the courage to define themselves in the relationship? What if Jerry had learned that family members could disagree about issues and still be loving and close? What if he had decided that it was more important to be a better version of himself than the one it took to win every argument? What if Doris had been brave enough to define her beliefs, even in the face of opposition? Would Kristen then have been able to calmly state her opinions without baiting her father? Might she have relinquished her desire to change her parents? What if they had decided that their relationship was based on something other than conformity?

There is a difference between telling people what *we* think and what *to* think. Defining self means that we consistently and calmly tell others what we think and feel, without demanding that they think and feel the same way. For example, many studies have revealed the profound influence of parents in the lives of their children and teenagers. However, many parents waste their influence by being too weak to share their positions with their children, or they coerce them into conformity and alienate them in the process.

When I (Trisha) was an older teenager, I talked to my father— a Baptist deacon—about the pressures I felt to get drunk and party with friends. He calmly listened to my fears about rejection and sympathized with me. Then he clarified his own position about the misuse of alcohol and the importance of good choices. He shared his dreams for my future and his own fears about my being hurt.

Until that night, I knew that my dad had prohibited my drinking alcohol and I knew that he did not want me to party with my friends. After that night, I knew why. Because he calmly listened to me without judging or arguing, I was able to listen to him articulate his position. Because he clearly outlined his value system in a reasonable way, I later used his arguments to bolster my own decision to abstain. Most importantly, though, I knew that my dad treasured his relationship with me even if I disagreed with him. There were times when Dad and I did have conflict, but that night stands out in my mind as a time when both of us were at our best, defining ourselves and allowing the other to do the same.

Give Up the Overfunctioning Position

When there is a job to be done, everyone loves an overfunctioner. Overfunctioners know the right way to do things (just ask them!), and they get things accomplished. They have high standards for themselves and they usually reach their goals. They also have high standards for everyone else and spend a great deal of energy making sure that others are doing what they should be. Overfunctioners, Gilbert says, talk more than they listen, give advice freely, and take responsibility for the feelings and choices of others.

Anywhere there is an overfunctioner, there is always an underfunctioner nearby. The underfunctioner may be a spouse who cannot quite get his act together or a child who just will not accept responsibility. If the overfunctioner is a pastor (and many are), the underfunctioning part of the equation might be a congregation that is more than happy to let the pastor do all the work. In one marriage, both partners took an extreme overfunctioning position but ended up with a cat who forgot how to clean itself—and eventually forgot how to walk—because it was so accustomed to having others take responsibility for meeting all its needs! Every overfunctioner requires an underfunctioner, which sets up the relationship to be an anxious one.

At first, the overfunctioning position seems to be the enviable one. In the church, we reward such people with accolades and admiration. An overfunctioning leader is even considered to be more spiritually effective and mature than others. As Lerner points out, "Everyone knows that chronic underfunctioners need to change. . . . In contrast, if we overfunction, we may truly believe that God is on our side." However, as with any anxiety-driven relationship pattern, the overfunctioner actually operates at the same level of differentiation of self as the underfunctioner, overfocusing on the needs, feelings, and choices of others and thus seeking distraction from a more appropriate, useful focus on self.

This sets up a difficult dilemma. The very behavior that is expected, and even demanded, of the leader in some congregations is exactly the behavior that leads to spiritual and emotional fatigue, burnout, and even physical illness. It sets the stage for family difficulties, as the minister is unable to relate to his or her family as an equal human being, sometimes strong and sometimes vulnerable, sometimes competent and sometimes inadequate. The ministerial image of adequacy may temporarily gain us respect in the church, but it robs us of intimacy and authenticity with our spouse and children.

When we begin to see and take responsibility for our part in the family's difficulties, we move from the overfunctioning position to one of equality. We begin to listen more and talk less. We are less compelled to tell people what they ought to think or feel or do. When we relate to our family, we step out of the role of pastor or leader. In fact, we realize that preaching (or playing therapist) at home does not help. Instead, we focus on building our connection with others and working on our own selves. We also learn to trust others to do the same.

When we relinquish the position of overfunctioning, we clear the way for our underfunctioning spouse and children to meet us halfway. Gilbert writes, in *Extraordinary Relationships*: "When the partners in this relationship are ready for equality of functioning, they can find ways to work toward it. If the overfunctioner will stop overfunctioning (that is, take responsibility for the self, and only for the self, communicate for the self and only for the self), often the underfunctioner can take the initiative for changing the relationship by changing the part that he or she contributes. This partner can begin to take responsibility for his or her self and for his or her decisions." However, we must remember that reducing our overfunctioning *in order to* force another person to stop underfunctioning is just another way of continuing to overfunction! Only when we stop focusing on the shortcomings of others can differentiation of self begin to take place.

Set Clear Boundaries

Everyone seems to have an instinctive need for good boundaries. For example, we understand the need for boundaries when we place a curtain in a window and when we lock the door. We expect these measures to define, for ourselves and for the world, what belongs to us and what we take responsibility for. We have expectations about ownership, privacy, and accountability. Boundaries within a family and between families and congregations serve the same important purposes.

In a well-functioning family, each person relates to every other person as a separate, distinct individual. Likewise, this kind of family unit relates to the larger system in the same well-defined way. Boundaries make this emotional separateness possible by providing lines of demarcation demonstrating what belongs to this person, to another, and to the family system.

Boundaries say, "What's mine is mine and what's yours is yours." They help us understand which feelings, decisions, thoughts, and principles belong to us and which belong to others. We see this delicate balance at work in the way our heavenly Father relates to us. In Scripture, he reveals himself and his love with clarity, inviting us to join him in his purposes. At the same time, he gives us the dignity of our own decisions, even our decisions about him, refusing to force or coerce us into compliance. When we clearly communicate our own boundaries and respect the boundaries of those we love, we are on our way to godly maturity.

Because a pastor is never truly off duty, it is easy for him or her to fall into a life with no boundaries. At home, we risk using our pastoral authority to trample on the boundaries of others. We may feel a need to control the values, decisions, and feelings of our spouses and children because we are afraid of how they will reflect on us. We may forget that we are the pastoral leader and that our family members are individuals in their own right, separate from our calling and ministry. At church, we risk failing to honor the legitimate boundaries of our family and ourselves because we fear the disapproval of church members or because we are emotionally invested in gaining their approval. Either way, we suffer, our family suffers, and even our congregation suffers.

First, we must learn to clearly communicate our own boundaries. We must learn to say, gently and firmly, "This is where I stand. This is who I am. This is what I will do and this is what I won't do. These are my feelings, values, and decisions." Sometimes, we may decide to explain our reasons; other times, we keep them to ourselves. However, we learn to refrain from being defensive or argumentative. We simply describe our position and then follow through. We may have to repeat ourselves, but we do not have to defend ourselves.

Visualizing the kind of boundaries we are attempting to establish can help us understand them better. A line on a tennis court is a boundary, and so are the walls of Fort Knox. Clearly, they are of different kinds and they have divergent functions. Personal and family boundaries should be clear and well-defined.

Abby, a young church staff member and ministry wife, said that she imagined her own boundaries as being like a chalk line on the ground that others ignored and disregarded, trespassing on her sense of self. As she matured, she came to see her personal boundary as a picket fence surrounding the house that represented her life. She noted that the fence was high enough, impossible to ignore, and hard to climb. The fence also had a gate in it, with the latch on the inside. As her mental picture of her life changed, so did her behavior with others.

Second, we begin to recognize how we accidentally or deliberately trespass the boundaries of others. We do this when:

- We do for others what they can and should do for themselves
- We demand that others conform to our way of thinking, instead of valuing both our similarities and our differences
- We consistently try to argue others out of their opinions or feelings
- We take responsibility for the feelings or decisions of others
- We try to control the behavior or responses of others (even when it is for their own good!)

Likewise, we respect the boundaries of our family members and our congregation when we:

- Agree to disagree and then move on
- Clearly communicate our own position while allowing others to do the same
- Take responsibility for our own ideas and decisions
- Welcome how others differ from us, seeking to learn from them
- Say no and set limits when appropriate
- Take care of our own needs whenever possible, without coercing others to take care of us

When we are clear about our own boundaries, we choose what we believe to be best for ourselves, our family, and our congregation without succumbing to the pressure of anxiety. We make decisions about family life on the basis of what is best for the family, not the preferences or expectations of the church. As a family, we seek to relate to the congregation as individuals with unique gifts and values rather than as a collective unit.

Develop a "Pause Button"

In his book *Man's Search for Meaning,* psychiatrist Victor Frankl describes the lessons he learned in a Nazi concentration camp. His most important realization was that although we cannot choose what happens to us, we can always choose how we respond to what happens to us. Drawing from his own painful experience, Frankl asserts that even when our lives are threatened, we can choose how we will die. No one, he says, not even a Nazi thug, can take that freedom to respond away from us.

Unfortunately, anxiety can. When we are anxious, we react to the pressures of the moment in a way that does not reflect our guiding principles. We do this because we give into our habitual behavior rather than pausing to think about other available options. This is why we must develop the ability to think before we speak and to pause before we act.

Stephen Covey applies this idea to our interaction with family members. "Obviously," he writes in *The 7 Habits of Highly Effective Families,* "family life would be a whole lot better if people acted based on their deepest values instead of reacting to the emotion or circumstance of the moment. What we all need is a 'pause button'— something that enables us to stop between what happens to us and our response to it, and to choose our response."

As family interactions become more intense, the pause button becomes more important. Sometimes it requires only a mental readjustment, reminding ourselves in the heat of the moment of our objectives or refocusing on our values. It may even be helpful to write down what we tend to forget and carry it in a pocket or post it on the refrigerator. A pastor wrote on his card, "Just because she has a different opinion doesn't mean she's attacking me." When things got tense at home, he would glance at his card and make a calm decision about how to respond to his wife.

Sometimes our commitment to pause requires us to let the other person know what we are doing. When anxiety is high and emotions are intense, we can hold our hands up and say, "Wait a minute, I need to slow down and think." This is a good time to reflect aloud on what is happening. Jennifer learned to do this when conflict with her teenaged daughter threatened to spin out of control, saying, "This is going too fast. I can't keep up. I think what you're saying is that it hurts your feelings when I won't loan you my car, because you think I don't trust you. Is that it?" Reflecting on the process together keeps us on the same side, confronting thorny issues rather than squared off on opposite sides of the issue. We have to be willing to do whatever it takes to slow things down, think about our options, and choose what is consistent with our values.

The Family Bank Account

Many theorists have suggested looking at family interactions by comparing them to a joint emotional bank account. Like all bank accounts, this shared emotional account depends on deposits and withdrawals. We make a deposit into this shared account when we engage in a positive interaction with each other and when we refrain from negative interaction. For example, when we offer encouraging words to someone, when we refrain from criticizing, when we spend time together, we deposit emotional currency in the family account.

Likewise, a withdrawal consists of a negative interaction or event that affects the family. Ignoring one another, exploding with anger, or using each other sexually all drain "money" from the family's emotional bank account. As with all bank accounts, the measure of success is simple: there must be more money going into the account than coming out. When the amount withdrawn exceeds the amount deposited, a family is emotionally overdrawn; over time, the family will be emotionally bankrupt.

During the early years of dating, engagement, and marriage, we are careful to make deposits into the relationship. We seek each other out, learn what pleases the other, pay attention to the other's needs and expectations. As time goes by, however, most couples become lazy about putting money into the emotional bank account. Distracted by the demands of life and anxious about the shortcomings in the relationship, they begin to take more and more money out of the bank account. Sometimes they make a large withdrawal when they engage in destructive, hurtful behavior. More often, they take money out of the bank in nickels and dimes through thoughtlessness or inattention. Some interactions, such as adultery or abuse, drain the account so quickly that the damage may be irreparable.

When a relationship is in trouble, there are only two ways to improve the account. Either we can figure out how to take less money out or we can focus on putting money in. It's as simple as that. Of course, simple is not the same thing as easy, and making changes in a marriage is rarely easy. Fortunately, any person in a family can decide at any time to change how he or she makes deposits into and withdrawals from the family's account. Though we must decide—and that is an essential first step—it is a vital connection to the life of Jesus and the desire to follow him in doing the right thing that motivates lasting change. Even if no one else in the family cooperates, the balance of the bank account can go up simply from the efforts of just one person.

When I (Trisha) use this concept to help a couple prevent or solve a problem in their marriage, I ask them to go through five steps:

1. Both the husband and the wife decide how much money they currently have in the joint emotional account. Sometimes one has a more negative opinion than the other. Rather than arguing about their opinions, I ask them instead to listen carefully to the other's perceptions and then find a compromise between the two. If the wife says tearfully that she believes the marriage is bankrupt, this is important information for the husband to hear, even if he sees it differently.

2. Both partners then answer the question, "What does my spouse do that puts money in the bank?" They are free to think of past contributions they have made as well as current ones. It is important to think of as many examples as they can.

3. The next question is more personal: "What do *I* do that takes money out of the bank?" Again, it is important to think of specific examples. This is not the time for excuses, explanation, or blaming. It is simply an opportunity to take responsibility for one's own part in the relationship.

4. The couple ask themselves, "What do *I* do that puts money into the bank?" When they have done this, they are ready for the last question: "As a couple, are we putting more money into the bank than we are taking out? If not, what are we going to do about it?"

5. Each person then makes a list of changes he or she is willing to initiate to put money into the bank or stop taking it out. This list is not shared with the spouse but is used to identify and motivate needed changes.

Notice that I do not ask the couple to identify what the spouse does to take money out of the bank. Typically, that is the focus of the relationship already, and a destructive one at that. There is time later for them to communicate with each other about their feelings on the other person's withdrawals, but that comes much later in the process. The starting place for transformation is always at the point of changing oneself, not the other.

The challenge of personal transformation is an exciting one. As we engage the journey of differentiation of self, we find many places to apply the understanding of leadership in a living system. Because interaction in the nuclear family is so intense and influences our lives and ministry so profoundly, it is one of the most challenging places to effect personal transformation. On the other hand, if transformation occurs here, it ripples out to all the other living systems in our lives.

Self-Assessment Questions

- As objectively as possible, identify the last experience of conflict you had in your nuclear family. Offering only the facts of what took place, avoiding blame and diagnosis, how would you describe it? Would the other parties involved agree with your presentation of the facts?
- Were you pleased with how the conflict turned out? Or was it simply a replay of a script the family has been through many times before? How would you think about revising your own role in that scene, if you could replay it now? How would you be different? What is your best guess about how the others would respond to your change?

- Which is the more difficult thing for you to do when the anxiety in your family rises: stay connected with the others or remain calm?
- What are you currently doing for someone else that the person should be doing for himself or herself?
- How would you describe the balance in the emotional bank account of your marriage? Write out your responses to the exercise in a journal.

Part Four

The Spirit and the Journey

Chapter Eight

The Spiritual Disciplines and the Path to Transformation

Superficiality is the curse of our age. The doctrine of instant satisfaction is a primary spiritual problem. The desperate need today is not for a greater number of intelligent people, or gifted people, but for deep people.
—RICHARD FOSTER, *CELEBRATION OF DISCIPLINE*

You've all been to the stadium and seen the athletes race. Everyone runs; one wins. Run to win. All good athletes train hard. They do it for a gold medal that tarnishes and fades. You're after one that's gold eternally. I do not know about you, but I'm running hard for the finish line. I'm giving it everything I've got. No sloppy living for me! I'm staying alert and in top condition. I'm not going to get caught napping, telling everyone else all about it and then missing out myself.
—ST. PAUL, 1 CORINTHIANS 9:24–27, *THE MESSAGE*

Jeff slumps further down into the overstuffed chair in my (Trisha's) office. A fellow pastor has recommended that Jeff enter therapy with me. "This is not why I went into ministry," he says flatly. "I didn't think I could change the world, but I did think I'd change a small part of it. Instead, I go from meeting to meeting trying to satisfy petty, demanding people. Something's got to change." As we talk, it becomes clear that Jeff is bored and run down. He blames his church members for his discontent, and he blames himself for not knowing how to turn things around. He is not clinically depressed, although he does have some of the symptoms. He is an effective pastor, but he feels like a failure. Jeff is on the verge of burnout.

I do not know Chris very well, so I am surprised when he puts his head down on his desk, sighs deeply, and then looks up with tears in his eyes. As the minister of education of a large church, Chris has been busy with church responsibilities all morning and is preparing to make announcements in the second worship service of the day. "I don't know what I'm going to do," he says. "The pastor requires that each staff member have at least one person ready to join the church in each worship service. I don't have anyone. If I don't find someone to join this church by eleven this morning, I'm dead meat."

I am certain that Chris did not follow God's call into ministry so he can meet membership quotas and please a domineering pastor. But that is exactly what his ministry has become.

"Soul Neglect"

None of us took on the sacrificial demands of leadership expecting to be buried in endless meetings and administrative details. We wanted meaningful ministry, supported by a rich and purposeful life, full of significance. Instead, we sometimes find ourselves busier than ever but going through the motions, with an emptiness clinging to our best efforts. Like Jeff, we know that something has to change. We may not be aware that what we crave is a supernatural transformation.

In his book *SoulShaping*, Douglas Rumford captures the essence of our dilemma: "Our search for something more out of life usually begins with externals. . . . We've confused activity with effectiveness, holding certain positions or titles with personal prestige, accumulating money with security, and sexual encounter with genuine intimacy. We've been so caught up in these pursuits that we haven't really considered what goals we are chasing—and what will happen when we actually catch them!"

Even leaders are not immune to looking for meaning in the externals. As the spiritual role model in the church, it is tempting to focus on what our lives look like, rather than on what is really going on inside. We measure our significance by the size of our congregation or by how well we are liked or by how highly we are thought of in the community. At workshops and seminars, we are offered a quick fix—three easy steps to church growth, five ways to reduce stress. Or we can buy books and tapes that promise to transform our ministry into a wildly successful one if we only try harder and follow the program. We obsess about the externals and starve our souls.

What Rumford calls "soul neglect" is a way of life for many in ministry. We grow busier and busier to please more and more people. We spend more time in meetings than we do in prayer. We scarcely have time to read the newspaper, much less spiritual classics or devotional readings. We study Scripture, but we do it for other people to convey God's Word to them. Our own hearts are often thirsty for a word from God, but who has time? We faithfully minister to the spiritual needs of others and teach ourselves to be content with the leftovers.

Our inattention to spiritual transformation first produces the fatigue, restlessness, and irritability that accompany burnout. Dissatisfied with our lives and ministry, we may feel melancholy or even hopeless. Some of us withdraw from responsibility and leadership, while others try to grasp the reins of the church more tightly. We may begin to hide from our dissatisfaction by immersing ourselves in mundane tasks and avoiding people, a strategy that drains the meaning from our ministry. Eventually, the spiritual malaise we experience creeps into the deepest part of our lives.

It is tempting to wonder, *Isn't that just the price we pay for being in leadership? Isn't that just the way things are?* Then we remember Jesus. Although he was certainly sensitive to the needs of others, the people pressing for his attention never determined his agenda. Jesus' emotional compass was not calibrated by the needs and demands of those around him. He never showed signs of boredom or disillusionment or spiritual disconnectedness. Instead, he regularly separated himself from the emotional intensity of his public life and aligned himself with the purpose of the Father (John 4:34). Only the redemptive plan of the Father determined for Jesus what the right thing was at any given moment.

As we saw in Chapter Two, the transformation we seek is the ability to do the right thing regardless of the pressure in our lives to do differently. We also saw that our own personal transformation comes only from our apprenticeship to Jesus, living as he lived and doing the things he did. The abstract question, "What would Jesus do?" gives way to the specific query, "What *did* Jesus do?" The Gospels are clear about what Jesus did: as he went about the normal life of an itinerant rabbi, Jesus prayed and fasted and read the Scriptures. He lived in intimate community, and he sought out regular times of solitude. He worshiped, lived simply, joined in celebrations, and served the needs of others.

In today's jargon, we would say that Jesus faithfully practiced an assortment of spiritual disciplines, cultivating a variety of "holy habits" that apparently defined him as surely as did his preaching and teaching. If we agree that imitating Jesus is the key to success as a Christian, why don't we do what he did?

Many leaders say they are too busy to practice the spiritual disciplines regularly. Some choose one or two with which they feel comfortable, without giving a passing thought to the others. (For an expanded list of the classical spiritual disciplines, see Appendix B). Others have felt drawn to practicing the disciplines but have stood silently watching from the sidelines, fearing the pain that comes from trying something different. Perhaps the reason we neglect forming these holy habits is that we are unaware of the power they have to change our lives.

"Holy Habits" and the Process of Transformation

Transformation does not come as we merely learn new skills or polish our image. Metamorphosis is a mysterious process that happens in a secret place. Painting wings on a caterpillar does not make a butterfly. Transformation of the human heart comes only through the Holy Spirit, and it comes only from the inside out. The disciplines carve out the pathways for the Spirit to work—what Siang-Yang Tan and Douglas Gregg call "the God-given means we are to use in our Spirit-filled pursuit of growing into the heart of God."

Our friend Steve Capper discovered this transforming power early in his ministry. Steve and his wife, Karen, began a discipline of weekly fasting on behalf of their young children, desiring them to develop their own relationships with God.

Soon, however, the practice began to change Steve significantly. "It was one method of hiding away in communion with the Lord,"

Steve says. "My hunger pangs reminded me that I was not hungry for success in ministry as we often define success but for intimacy with the Lord." During difficult times in the ministry and in the family, Steve and Karen continued their weekly fast. "I realized that while I have no choice about being anointed in terms of a widely influential public ministry, I *do* have a choice about being yielded to God for a depth of influence with those God had given me. And," Steve adds, "I finally realized that who I am, including who I am in Christ, matters more than what I do in ministry."

In the parable of the sower, Jesus compares the process of spiritual growth to the growth of healthy plants after seed is sown. Whether a seed takes root and grows depends on the quality of the soil in which it is planted.

We cannot make the seed grow; we don't even plant it. We are responsible for the condition of the soil. We prepare the soil for the mysterious work of God by the practice of spiritual disciplines. On our way to worship one Sunday morning, my children and I (Trisha) passed a man walking on the sidewalk of our quiet residential street. Dressed in an expensive hiking outfit and boots, he shouldered a large, heavy backpack and bedroll and carried a sturdy walking stick. Both my children commented on how unusual he looked, walking through the neighborhood carrying so much gear. I explained to them that the man was clearly "in training," building strength and endurance for a future event when the demands would be more rigorous than the sidewalks of our suburban street.

Like the hiker's backpack and gear, the spiritual disciplines help us build up our spiritual muscles so that when life requires more of us, we can rise to the task. We are able to build mature spiritual responses into our lives even before we need them. As Rumford writes, "Discipline develops the reflexes in our souls."

This means that the pastor who has faced his own fear of failure in times of solitude is less afraid when a family threatens to leave the church. The minister who has discerned the will of God for her church through soul-searching prayer is less at the mercy of others' agendas. The disciplines help us train to live the kind of life we truly want to live. Regular practice of a variety of spiritual disciplines also helps us be the kind of leader we want to be: mature, well-differentiated, and focused.

The Spiritual Disciplines and Differentiation of Self

The emotional and spiritual maturity that we are calling differentiation of self does not happen by accident. It is not enough to want to be mature or to learn a way of appearing mature to others. True maturity comes from pursuing "training in godliness" (1 Timothy 4:7). This is the role of the spiritual disciplines in our lives.

Unfortunately, sinful reactions are built into our human nature. We are hardwired to react to others in a destructive and self-serving way. That is, it is easier for us to react sinfully than it is to choose to respond otherwise. Paul spoke of this in Romans 7 as sin embodied in the flesh. Even when we want to do good, we often find it easier to act sinfully, imprisoned by the "law of sin" at work in our bodies (Romans 7:15–24).

This automatic, emotional reactivity is what must be modified if we are to function with a higher level of differentiation. Paul makes it clear in Romans 8 that only the indwelling, powerful work of the Holy Spirit can overcome the automatic reactions of sinful nature. Good intentions can't, wishful thinking can't, even willpower can't. This is where the spiritual disciplines come in.

Spiritual disciplines are the means by which these automatic reactions are ultimately changed. The disciplines work to rewire our automatic reaction, offering us options about how to respond in a given situation. We no longer *have* to react as we once did. In fact, practicing the spiritual disciplines helps us see ourselves and the rest of the system with clarity and divinely guided insight so that we can make our choice on the basis of God's revealed truth rather than from the pressures brought to bear on us by the system.

The ability to do the right thing even when under pressure to do otherwise begins with the ability to separate ourselves from the emotional intensity and chaos of our relationships so that we can make a well-reasoned choice. By physically withdrawing and seeking solitude with God, we open ourselves to the perspective of the Holy Spirit, a perspective that is often drowned out by the distractions of everyday life. As we quiet our inner selves through Christian meditation, we become more aware of the distinction between our emotions and our beliefs. It usually takes me (Trisha) at least fifteen minutes of quiet reflection just to begin to untangle the cacophony of competing feelings and thoughts and reach a place where I can calmly consider the options before me. When I am under stress, it may take much longer.

Chronic anxiety can also be diluted by regular practice of spiritual disciplines. Meditation, of course, is physically and emotionally calming, but the spiritual benefits are more profound. In Christian meditation, the focus shifts from anxiety-driven behavior (doing) to spiritual insight (being) as we concentrate on the character of God and the words of Scripture.

In such a time of intentional quiet, solitude, and contemplation, we remember that we are more interested in pleasing God than in pleasing others, and that we desire to conform to his will for our lives even if this means disappointing those close to us. We allow our heavenly Father to remind us of our utter dependence on him, minimizing our tendency to relate to others as if we were dependent on them for approval or acceptance.

"I cannot meditate. I cannot even think. My head is so noisy," a student minister said to me (Trisha) as we talked about the anxiety swirling around her ministry. Journaling helped her externalize the anxiety so she could examine it and manage the emotional chaos. A commitment to celebration (also a spiritual discipline!) is a meaningful way to cultivate playfulness, which is a valuable antidote to chronic anxiety.

The Psalms often show us the journey from anxiety to peace that unfolds when we offer ourselves to God in prayer. In Psalm 73, for example, the psalmist challenges God with the unfairness of a world in which the wicked prosper. After pouring out a litany of complaints, the psalmist remembers the presence and blessing of God in his own life and begins to break free from his overwhelming envy. He eventually is able to proclaim, "My flesh and my heart may fail, but God is the strength of my heart and my portion forever" (Psalm 73:26). Through the holy habit of prayer and the corresponding discipline of writing it down, the psalmist finds deep personal strength and changed perspective.

Implementing the spiritual disciplines in our lives also helps us minimize our anxious reactivity and choose a more constructive response instead. For example, the practice of studying the Scriptures brings the cognitive perspective to an emotionally laden situation. We are reminded by the words on the page to love our enemy even when our natural reaction is to lash out in hatred. As we pray for our enemy, we open ourselves up to consider compassion and mercy. As we confess our sins, we face our own sinfulness and avoid overfocusing on the sinfulness of the other. Gradually, we experience transformation, becoming the kind of people who are actually capable of forgiving an enemy.

Our friend Steve (mentioned earlier) began experimenting with the disciplines of solitude and silence. Sometime later, he received an unkind, manipulative e-mail from a church member. Feeling hurt, Steve read the message twice and then angrily hit the delete key. "Then," he reflects, "I literally walked away for about twenty minutes, intentionally seeking just the briefest period of solitude. I remembered what a friend had said, that 'the hardest thing for me to see is me,' so I began to pray through Psalm 139, asking God to show me my own heart and my part in this. Once I began to feel peace, I returned to the computer. I thought, 'You are my brother in Christ and you deserve a response.'" Steve was able to respond to the criticism thoughtfully and prayerfully, avoiding a potentially destructive reaction.

Beginning to Live a Disciplined Life

So, now what? Most of us in ministry already believe that we should pray more, study more, read more, worship more. That knowledge and the guilt that goes with it rarely change our behavior for long. We will change only when we believe that the hard work of enlarging our spiritual capacity is more important than improving the externals.

It is human nature to work diligently to get the externals in place and then use God to prop them up. We look to see how others can meet our needs, and then we pray for God to use them to do so. We determine what it will take for others to like and respect us and we ask God to help us with the task. We focus on what is seen—our image, our reputation, our results, even our religious regimen—and completely miss what is unseen.

In his classic book *Celebration of Discipline,* Richard Foster reminds us that the spiritual disciplines are uniquely designed by God to allow us to receive His grace by allowing "us to place ourselves before God so that He can transform us . . . We must always remember that the path does not produce the change; it only puts us in the place where the change can occur." But first, we must get on the path.

Start Where You Are

The starting line for authentic change is where we are, not where we are not. Several years ago, I (Trisha) found myself being drawn to some of the contemplative disciplines not commonly taught in my denomination. I went to seminars and on retreats to learn how to practice centering prayer and contemplative meditation but found myself completely unable to practice the disciplines at home. Fidgety and restless, I would sit miserably, trying to focus or trying not to focus, but utterly unable to pray. I was ready to give up. After some time, a friend suggested to me, "Continue to set aside the time with God, but stop trying to pray. Just sit in the presence of God."

So I got up early every morning and sat on the sofa in the living room. I would verbally acknowledge the presence of God, saying, "I know that you are here. I know that you are closer to me than the air I breathe, and in You I live and move and have my very being. I am here to rest in your presence. I love you." Then I would sit. Nothing very spiritually exciting ever happened. Some mornings I fell asleep. But the holy habit of sitting quietly in the presence of God had begun to take root in my life, setting the stage for later development of centering prayer and quiet meditation. By trying too hard, I was setting myself up to fail. When I began where I was, I laid a foundation on which to build.

Begin with a Journal

Often, successful pursuit of spiritual discipline begins with a journal. In fact, Douglas Rumford calls use of a journal "the secret to getting beyond good intentions." In *Too Busy Not to Pray*, pastor Bill Hybels describes his skepticism about the practical value of journaling: "I had visions of people who would spend hours and hours . . . just letting their stream of consciousness flow all over endless reams of paper. I thought to myself, 'Anyone who has time to do that kind of thing is not my kind of guy. Don't people have anything better to do with their time?'"

Eventually, however, Hybels followed a simple plan for keeping a journal. Each day, he wrote the word "Yesterday" on a page in a spiral notebook. Then, limiting himself to only one page, he wrote about the events of the previous day. "Most of us . . . lead unexamined lives. We repeat the same errors day after day. We do not learn much from the decisions we make. One benefit of journaling is to force us to examine our lives."

Hybels then began to write his prayers for the day, again limiting himself to one page. He writes that his first journal entry read, "Yesterday I said I hated the concept of journals and I had strong suspicions about anyone who has the time to journal, and I still do, but if this is what it is going to take to slow me down so I can learn to talk and walk with Christ the way I should, I'll journal." Despite this skeptical beginning, he enthusiastically affirms the importance of this discipline that enriched his prayer life and changed his character.

I (Trisha) discovered the power of journaling as a teenager when I learned that writing my prayers focused my mind and sharpened my sense of God's presence. The process of writing slows me down and prevents me from moving too fast in my relationship with God. I later learned to use my journal to listen to God, writing down what I thought God was saying to me through Scripture and through the inner voice of the Holy Spirit. As a pastoral counselor, I now encourage almost all my clients to keep a journal, even if they only write in it occasionally. A journal is a window into our soul, illuminating our feelings and motives. It offers a place to explore our beliefs and values so that we can determine whether we are living consistently with them. Most important, the habit of reflection that a journal cultivates is often the first step toward learning to see the invisible.

Practice the Presence of God

Most of us are very good at living our lives in "parts." There is the part of our attention we devote to our family, and the part we give to our work. Another part goes to leisure time, and still another part is devoted to our spiritual life. No wonder we feel so fragmented so much of the time.

The spiritual disciplines work against this temptation to compartmentalize our life. By praying, fasting, meditating, retreating, or celebrating, we remind ourselves of the constant, pervasive nearness of God. Rather than assigning to God a part of our day, we teach ourselves to notice God at work throughout the day. In *Your God Is Too Safe,* Mark Buchanan writes, "The problem is not that God is distant and needs to be wooed or badgered into coming near; the problem is that God is ever present, ever near, and that some of us seek ways of escape. . . . God does not need to be invoked, we do. We need to be called to our senses, to be as present to God as God is to us." This is why we practice the spiritual disciplines.

In my pursuit of a reflective life, I (Jim) came to the realization that I operated much of every day on autopilot. In an attempt to obey the admonition to "pray without ceasing" (1 Thessalonians 5:17), I began to practice what one friend called a "holy pause." I actually put into my schedule each day several fifteen-minute pauses. I use that time to reflect on what has transpired in the previous several hours, looking for the activity of God. I look ahead to the next several hours and pray for a constant awareness of the Father's presence in all of my activities and appointments. As I practice this faithfully over a season, I develop a greater capacity to actually live with a prayer consciousness consistently.

Buchanan points out that it is such holy habits that allow us to maintain awareness of God's nearness even when he seems far away, to "practice the presence of God, to train ourselves to hold still, to run toward Him, not away, to have the scales fall from our eyes, and always, everywhere, to behold Him. . . . When we practice the presence of God, we train ourselves to desire His presence—to resist our temptation to flee Him. We also train ourselves to experience His presence—to resist our temptation to think that He flees us."

Work with Your Temperament

Not all of us are contemplative by nature. Some of us are action-oriented, not reflective, and many of the spiritual disciplines do not seem to fit our lifestyle or us. My (Trisha's) husband, Craig, walks when he prays. Nowadays, he paces, but in our first house, he prayed late at night, walking circles from the kitchen, through the living room, the foyer, the den, and back to the kitchen. There was nothing contemplative about his praying—it was vigorous and energetic—but it was spiritual and it was disciplined.

We must resist the temptation to take on the spiritual disciplines in cookie-cutter fashion, trying to conform to the experience of others. Some leaders find it easy to fast, while others cannot imagine even trying. Some find solitude to be soothing and comfortable; some find their stride as they serve the practical needs of others. The spiritual disciplines offer us a variety of paths to enlarge our spiritual lives and heighten our experience of God's grace. Although the disciplines require that we regularly take on activities that are neither easy nor comfortable for us, we do not all need to travel the same path, or all travel it the same way.

Set Out as an Amateur

At the same time, we must remember that anything worth doing is worth doing badly! Many of us avoid practicing unfamiliar disciplines because we shun anything we cannot already do well. As professionals, we are accustomed to feeling competent in our spiritual lives. Experimenting with the spiritual disciplines requires taking on amateur status. We trade professional self-sufficiency for a learning curve. The bad news is that this exchange leaves us feeling uncertain and inept. The good news is that this is exactly where God's grace takes over and transformation occurs.

In the spring of 2000, I (Robert) undertook a new practice that has proved as helpful as it has been difficult to sustain. Sensing a need for a regular and extended time of solitude and prayer to perform the tasks of a pastor with integrity, I began to schedule a monthly day of prayer at a local retreat center. Guarding that day against the inevitable attempts at intrusion, I have been able to enjoy about eight or nine such days a year.

I usually begin the day by reading and praying from the Psalms and seeking to become aware of God's presence. I then take my journal and write down as much as I can of what is on my mind, troubling me, stirring my anxiety. Writing it down helps me to objectify it and get it out of the way for a while. My intent is to clear my own agenda and be able to hear God's voice through Scripture and prayer. Often, about midmorning, I meet with a retreat director for an hour or so to talk about what I've brought to the day in the way of needs and expectations, and to receive some guidance about how the remainder of the day might best be spent.

Most days of prayer like these include a long walk, a short nap, and some spiritual reading from writers such as Henri Nouwen, Eugene Peterson, and Richard Foster. Around 4:00 P.M., I end the day by writing again, gathering the thoughts and directions of the day into the pages of my journal.

Nothing profound has come from any of these days over the past couple of years. Some would look upon them as a waste of time, time that ought to have been spent in a hundred other more visible activities.

But something profound has come from the accumulation of all those days. I have learned more about being still and trusting God to work in my life, my family, and my congregation. I have learned that the other work of the pastorate is going to get done, regardless. But prayer is not attended to unless I create space for it in my life. I have learned that no one is going to check up on me and see if I am giving time to prayer; I, nevertheless, need to do so. I have learned that away from the voices and noises of the congregation it is easier to take a more objective look at what is transpiring and to enter it with a greater degree of peace and calmness that has come from taking hold of God's hand in prayer and solitude. By practicing the spiritual disciplines regularly and faithfully, I have seen God begin to transform my life from the inside out.

Prepare for an Adventure

The spiritual disciplines are meant to lead us out into the unknown, away from the predictable life of committee meetings and building campaigns and membership goals. They beckon us into the unfamiliar and lead us on a solitary voyage toward the heart of God. We are tempted to use them like a spiritual Franklin Planner to help us master our lives; in fact, they are intended to help us relinquish control to the transforming work of the Holy Spirit within our lives.

For such a quest, we need companions. We need the fellowship of those who have traveled the path before us. We need the wisdom of those who know from experience what lies ahead. We need the camaraderie of fellow adventurers. As we will see in the next chapter, we cannot make this journey alone.

Self-Assessment Questions

- How would you describe the purpose of practicing spiritual disciplines? What keeps it from becoming empty ritual or simple asceticism?
- List the spiritual disciplines you find present in the life of Jesus as described in the New Testament Gospels. Why do you think he engaged in these practices?
- How do you think the practice of spiritual disciplines helps a person grow forward in differentiation of self?
- What spiritual practices would you like to see most consistently practiced in your own life? What changes would be necessary to get to that point?
- Which disciplines are easiest for you to engage? Which are most difficult? Why?

Chapter Nine

Learning Communities

We now live in a time when consumer Christianity has become the accepted norm, and all-out engagement with and in Jesus' kingdom among us is regarded as somewhat "overdoing it." By contrast, the biblical pattern is, from beginning to end, "Be ye doers of the word, and not hearers only."
—DALLAS WILLARD, *THE DIVINE CONSPIRACY*

I do not want any of you sitting around on your hands. I do not want anyone strolling off, down some path that goes nowhere. And mark that you do this with humility and discipline—not in fits and starts, but steadily, pouring yourselves out for each other in acts of love, alert at noticing differences and quick at mending fences.
—ST. PAUL, EPHESIANS 4:2–3, *THE MESSAGE*

"I don't get it," Jorge said. The discouragement in his voice was noticeable. It was his fifth lunch meeting in seven months with another pastor from the area. They had been sharing their struggles in ministry and agreed to serve as accountability partners. "I've tried so hard. My intentions were so good. I've set specific goals and I've been relentlessly honest—but I don't see much progress. Maybe I just cannot change."

Jorge's experience is like that of many pastors who are often quick to acknowledge the need for their own personal transformation. The acknowledgment is immediately followed with the question, "How?"

We understand Jorge's dilemma. The Apostle Paul articulates it clearly:

> It happens so regularly that it is predictable. The moment I decide to do good, sin is there to trip me up. I truly delight in God's commands, but it is pretty obvious that not all of me joins in that delight. Parts of me covertly rebel, and just when I least expect it, they take charge. I've tried everything and nothing helps. I'm at the end of my rope. Is there no one who can do anything for me? Isn't that the question? The answer, thank God, is that Jesus Christ can and does. He acted to set things right in this life of contradictions where I want to serve God with all my heart and mind, but am pulled by the influence of sin to do something totally different [Romans 7:14–20, *The Message*].

Is there a way that pastors who want to make change in their lives can actually do so? Is it possible to embrace the ways of thinking that we are suggesting and overcome the probability of another failed attempt at change?

Honesty requires us to acknowledge that nothing is more difficult than changing lifelong habits. Learning to know and do the right things more consistently is an enormous goal for a leader. Leading a complex living system is deeply challenging. Learning to think systems and see process requires hard work. Understanding triangles in human relationships and engaging appropriate moves to detriangle demands courage and patience. Establishing the practices of a reflective life that foster these abilities requires Herculean effort. This raises the question, "Is it possible to really change the fundamental habits and relationships in our lives?"

Honesty also requires us to declare the truth: "I can do all things through Christ who strengthens me" (Philippians 4:13). Paul's words are encouraging: "God can do anything, you know—far more than you could ever imagine or guess or request in your wildest dreams! He does it not by pushing us around but by working within us, his Spirit deeply and gently within us. Glory to God in the Church down through all generations" (Ephesians 3:20, *The Message*).

The Scripture declares that change—difficult though it may be—is possible.

Effective leaders dramatically increase the likelihood of change when they create a learning community that embraces the values of grace giving and truth telling. In this chapter, we describe the process embraced by an effective learning community and suggest some key players in that community.

The Process of Learning

How we approach personal change often contributes to our failure. In *The Divine Conspiracy*, Willard suggests that we should "at least consider the possibility that this poor result is not in spite of what we teach and how we teach, but precisely because of it." In our culture, learning has become synonymous with possessing information or giving intellectual assent. As important as each of these is, they are not enough to produce behavioral change. Knowing the correct answer is not the same as doing the right thing. In our experience, those who achieve change do not embrace a formula or a program. They commit to a process that provides simple guidance in the midst of the complexity of seeking personal transformation. The process is a continuous cycle of information, practice, and reflection.

Jesus, the master teacher, consistently engaged this model. He openly shared his life with his followers. Using parables and sermons, he taught them basic concepts of kingdom living (Matthew 5–7). He sent them out to practice what they had been learning (Luke 10:1–16). When they returned from their practice sessions, he reflected with them on their learning and rejoiced with them in their accomplishment (Luke 10:17–24).

Information: Master the Concepts

Those who desire the personal transformation described in this book will begin by mastering the concepts. Changing our way of thinking is not as easy as flipping a light switch; habits are thoroughly ingrained. Serious students of change spend time reading various authors in the field of living systems. With each new reading, another level of understanding emerges.

Living systems theory has its own language. Some resist the new language, but it reinforces the need for new behavior. Test yourself by reflecting on these seven concepts; how well could you describe and illustrate them without the help of written notes?

1. Differentiation of self
2. Togetherness forces
3. Anxiety
4. Triangling
5. Overfunctioning
6. Family of origin
7. Thinking systems, watching process

Reading a variety of authors who express these concepts with slightly different nuance helps bring richness and depth to the student's understanding of the concepts. In the Bibliography and the Recommended Reading list, we offer suggestions for your reading.

But mastering the concepts is about more than having intellectual knowledge. It is about examining yourself—your beliefs and convictions—to determine if this way of understanding reality fits your view of how life really is. This requires theological reflection. It leads you to examine the beliefs that were given to you in your earliest spiritual formation.

Dallas Willard encourages this kind of reflection. He writes (again in *The Divine Conspiracy*), "It is one of the major transitions of life to recognize who has taught us, mastered us, and then to evaluate the results in us of their teaching. This is a harrowing task, and sometimes we just can not face it. But it can open the door to choose other masters, possibly better masters, and one Master above all."

Theological reflection will lead you to examine the life of Jesus and the teachings of Paul and other New Testament writers to see if this way of thinking reflects your own understanding of Scripture.

I (Jim) serve as pastor of Harbor Church, a network of house churches in Houston's inner city. Harbor Church has a one-year leadership development process for potential church planters. In the early stages of the process, we teach the concepts of the living system. Participants are required to read at least two books that use these concepts (and they are asked to demonstrate intellectual mastery of the key concepts that are in the Glossary of this book). They demonstrate mastery by meeting regularly with an accountability group in which they are asked to define key terms from their reading, in their own words. This does not ensure changed behavior, but it does begin to assist in internalizing the concepts.

Practice: Engage in New Behaviors

For personal transformation to occur, we must identify behavior that we desire to change in light of the new information. We live in an information age, and in Western culture we are deceived into believing that if we can intellectually understand a concept, we have learned it.

Ultimately, however, learning is about changing our behavior. So in this second phase of the cycle, I may discover that I most often deal with anxiety in relationships by overfunctioning. I then decide that I don't want to continue to deal with my anxiety in this way. I ask myself: "What behaviors should I consider changing in light of this new information? What new behaviors or disciplines do I need to take on if I am to see this change occur?" Asking and answering questions of this sort presses us into further learning.

As the new behavior that is desired becomes clear, the leader must practice the behavior. This requires some level of risk. By definition you are a novice at the new behavior, and all novices experience failure. This is at the heart of the learning process.

It is helpful for the adult learner to recognize that learning moves through a series of stages. Learning any new behavior is like learning to ride a bicycle. Until we see someone riding one, we are *unconsciously incompetent;* we do not know how to ride one and we do not know that we cannot. Once we see someone cruising effortlessly down the road on a ten-speed, however, things change. We become *consciously incompetent.* We now know two things: there is such a thing as a bicycle, and we do not know how to ride one. At the next stage of learning we become *consciously competent.* We have to focus hard on balancing, steering, and pedaling. We give all our attention to the task, and although we do not present an elegant example, we are doing it. Over time, our muscles and brains learn the new skills. Eventually, we cruise effortlessly down the road, *unconsciously competent,* doing without thinking the thing we once could not do at all.

So it is with these new behaviors of a living system. As soon as we identify new behavior, we become conscious of our incompetence.

During the practice session, we work at the level of conscious competence. Given time and disciplined effort, the new behavior becomes part of our unconscious competence.

Leaders who stay engaged through the discomfort of the conscious competence stage reap significant rewards.

Once the participants in Harbor Church's leadership development process have demonstrated intellectual mastery of the living-systems concepts, they are asked to take the next step. They identify two relationships—one with a member of their family of origin and one with an unchurched person. The family relationship is one in which the participants recognize the anxiety-driven reactiveness they would like to change. In addition, we find that many followers of Christ experience and express a great deal of anxiety in seeking to relate to people who do not share their faith and practices.

For six months, participants are asked to regularly establish a face-to-face meeting with the people in each relationship. The specific goal is to remain differentiated while increasing connection. First, participants identify and describe the anxious behavior they observe in themselves as they engage each relationship. Then they describe how they want to behave differently. Finally, they regularly connect to each person and attempt to practice the new behavior.

Assignments of this kind are based on the belief that change comes best when we identify the behavior we want to adjust and ask a community that is full of grace and truth to support us and hold us accountable for making the changes. This kind of exercise is a powerful learning experience because it brings the participants face to face with themselves. Participants experience how they allow their immature anxious reactions to reduce their ability to live their conviction in these important relationships. Through practice, they also develop other habits in these relationships, learning to handle old difficulties in a new way. This awareness increases the possibility of living responsibly.

Reflection: What Did You Learn?

A leader who practices the new behavior intended to increase differentiation and reduce anxious response inevitably fails. The failure produces a new round of anxiety. To diminish the power of that cycle, the leader must build in time for reflection. Here are some ways to use reflection time:

- Ask yourself: *How did I do? At what points was I successful? What happened in the conversation that triggered old behavior? What could I do differently next time?*
- Describe the experience to another person and ask for feedback.
- Go back to some of the living-systems literature to refresh your memory and clarify your understanding.
- Engage the spiritual disciplines during this time and seek guidance and strength from the Holy Spirit. Ask him to renew your resolve and to empower your change efforts.

The information that comes from this reflective process prepares the leader to go back to the relationships and practice some more. Continue to repeat the cycle until you begin to master the practice.

In Harbor Church's leadership development process, after each contact with the member of the family of origin and the unchurched person, participants debrief the experience with a coach and with a peer group. By sharing new insights and awareness with their peers and coaches, they create an environment of accountability that fosters growth and learning. Describing both their successes and their failures enhances self-understanding.

Using living-systems terminology, participants reflect on how their key relationships are working. They identify ongoing goals for behavior change and map out the next meeting with each key relationship. Each participant is challenged to set aside significant time of solitude to reflect on how the relationship is working and to seek God's guidance in the next steps to take.

Establishing a Learning Community

Leaders who want to experience the personal transformation called for in this book establish a community in which they are supported *and* held accountable for making the desired changes.

We live in a culture that continues to embrace a mental model of the self-sufficient leader who knows all the answers and who single-handedly deals with all of life's challenges.

In *The Fifth Discipline,* Peter Senge observes:

> Our traditional views of leaders—as special people who set the direction, make the key decisions, and energize the troops—are deeply rooted in an individualistic and nonsystemic worldview. Especially in the West, leaders are *heroes*—great men (and occasionally women) who "rise to the fore" in times of crises. Our prevailing leadership myths are still captured by the image of the captain of the cavalry leading the charge to rescue the settlers from attacking Indians. So long as such myths prevail, they reinforce a focus on short-term events and charismatic heroes rather than on systemic forces and collective learning. At its heart, the traditional view of leadership is based on assumptions of people's powerlessness, their lack of personal vision and inability to master the forces of change, deficits which can be remedied only by a few great leaders.

Leaders often live with the illusion that new skills and behaviors can be achieved by an effort of will and hard work. To be sure, engaging one's will and working hard are essential. But that is not enough. The Christian faith boldly and counterculturally invites us to live with transparency and authenticity in a community of grace and truth (1 John 1:5–7; James 5:16).

Intentionally fostering a learning community is a key element for a successful transformation journey. This community should embrace the cycle of learning we have described, and it should hold core values of grace and truth where participants learn to effectively speak the truth in love (John 1:12–14; Ephesians 4:11–16). Such a community is most likely to foster change, allowing the leader the safety to reflect on the nature and quality of his or her leadership.

Engaging community at this level of transparency is challenging. Most pastors have little or no experience with such a community. Those who know pastors best consistently describe the loneliness and sense of isolation that characterizes the pastoral community. Many pastors live in an overfunctioning position with their congregation. When they attempt to step back to become more intentionally equal in posture and more reflective, the congregation often engages in a variety of anxious behaviors designed (intentionally or unintentionally) to restore the pastor to the overfunctioning position. They insist that the pastor change back!

As you consider taking initiative to create a community filled with grace and truth that embraces the information, practice, reflection cycle, we suggest that you consider four specific sets of relationships.

Find a Coach

Jesus built his life's ministry around a coaching relationship with twelve men. He taught them; he modeled the behaviors he wanted them to engage; he gave them feedback about their behavior. Ultimately, all but one of them became competent practitioners of these behaviors.

Every leader could benefit from a relationship with a coach who is outside the congregational system. This person could be another pastor from the area, a trusted church consultant, a pastoral counselor, a family systems therapist, a denominational leader, or a mature and wise older friend.

The leader seeking a coach should look for at least three characteristics. First, the coach should have a clear mental model of change. Serving as a successful pastor and coaching another leader through personal transformation are two different skill sets. Coaching a person who seeks personal transformation is about more than being a good friend or supportive colleague. As valuable as this support is, it is not enough to foster transformation. A leader who is seeking a coach would be well served to ascertain with clarity the potential coach's understanding and practice of personal transformation.

Second, the coach should have a credible track record of engaging in long-term relationships that reflect a substantial ability to remain less anxious in a congregational system. No leader is nonanxious. We all experience anxiety throughout life. Some pastors spend their entire ministry moving from place to place, never facing the anxiety in and around them. They miss the learning that could move them to a higher level of emotional maturity. When seeking a coach, the leader should obtain personal evidence that the coach has some level of mastery in this skill.

Third, the coach should be able to commit adequate time to the relationship. Personal transformation is a lifelong process with intensive seasons that require concentrated attention. The leader should have some level of assurance that the one engaged as a coach can sustain the commitment to the relationship.

Establish a Peer Group

Peer learning is a powerful tool being used in many circles today. Reggie McNeal notes, in *A Work of Heart:* "A critical intellectual capacity for twenty-first century leadership success will be the ability to build knowledge together with other colleagues. The rate of information growth, coupled with the collapse of the Christendom paradigm, makes it no longer possible to prepare for ministry challenge through traditional preparation processes. Academic, conferential, and self-guided learning must be supplemented through a peer mentoring process for debriefing life and ministry experiences."

Peer learning can take on many faces. It can be a place for learning new preaching skills or for reflecting on the experience of leading change in the congregation. It can be a place for learning communication skills in marriage. In the context of personal transformation, it takes on a supportive role that gives an individual a variety of perspectives through which core beliefs can be clarified, anxious behavior identified, and nonreactivity rehearsed and reported upon (Proverbs 11:14).

Basic ground rules of a peer learning group, such as schedule, confidentiality, and full participation, should be observed. Additionally, three requirements should be considered in the context of this form of peer learning. First, if possible, the group should have a facilitator. This individual should have some experience with applying living-systems concepts. He or she stands apart from the group as a differentiated but connected presence who observes process and coaches the group as it develops. Second, each participant should commit to mastering the concepts of the living system. In the early stages of the process, the group should engage learning exercises that allow group members to demonstrate this mastery. Third, each participant should regularly bring a case study for the group to consider.

We offer one word of caution. Personal support groups have proliferated in our culture. These can be helpful, but the leader must be careful that support does not foster the togetherness force in a manner that discourages differentiation.

Tim was a pastor in the Houston area—intelligent, effective, and sincerely devoted to God. I (Jim) encountered him one day at a meeting of pastors. We were friends, so I was aware that he had been under a good deal of stress. His mother was slowly dying of cancer and he was faithfully caring for her. At the same time his congregation was in the midst of building a new sanctuary. As I prepared to go to the meeting, I picked up a set of movie passes to give to Tim. I wanted to encourage him to take care of himself.

When I saw him in the hallway at the meeting, I handed him the passes and he began to weep. The simple act of kindness uncorked a load of stress. We quickly found a quiet place and for the next hour he unloaded the weight of the burden he was carrying.

That conversation became the impetus for formation of the first peer group in which I had ever participated. It was not a group about family systems, but it became a group in which a set of trusted peers embraced the values of grace and truth. Though that group eventually concluded, the impact on my life has been profound. The group was a safe place for me to explore a variety of behavior changes that I wanted to make in my life and ministry. It was a new experience for me to get honest feedback about my behavior from friends who were personally committed to my success.

Form a Vision Community

Ultimately, a congregation is a highly complex human social system. Clearly, a change in the leader's behavior brings about change in the system. The help of a coach and a peer learning group from outside the congregational system strengthens the process of transformation. Ultimately, the leader increases the effective functioning of the congregation if a core group of key leaders understands and embraces the ability to function as well-differentiated leaders.

In *Generation to Generation,* Ed Friedman observed the importance of having emotionally and spiritually healthy people leading a congregation:

> The overall health and functioning of any organization depends primarily on . . . the people at the top, and that is true whether the relationship system is a personal family, a sports team, an orchestra, a

congregation, a religious hierarchy, or an entire nation. The reason for that connection is not some mechanistic, trickle-down, domino effect. It is, rather, that leadership . . . is essentially an organic, perhaps even biological, phenomenon. And an organism tends to function best when its "head" is well differentiated. The key to successful spiritual leadership, therefore, with success understood not only as moving people toward a goal, but also in terms of the survival of the family (and its leader), has more to do with the leaders' capacity for self-definition than with the ability to motivate others.

An effective vision community needs to be a group of such leaders.

Forming a vision community committed to personal transformation increases the likelihood of a leader's success in bringing about personal transformation. The impact is felt both personally and corporately.

In *Leading Congregational Change,* coauthors Mike Bonem and James Furr and I (Jim) defined a vision community as "a diverse group of key members who become a committed and trusting community in order to discern and implement God's vision for the congregation. The vision community should be a part of the change process from beginning to end. Its members must become personally prepared, understand and clearly feel the sense of urgency, and agree that change is needed."

The chances that a personal transformational journey will lead to congregational transformation are greatly increased if the key leaders share that vision and embrace the journey themselves.

Stay Connected to Jesus

In the second chapter of this book, we hold Jesus up as the model of a mature, differentiated person. His exceptional life is the one that we turn to for inspiration, instruction, and correction. Failure to keep his life in the center of our vision results in the other components of the learning community becoming just another self-help process. But if he is in the midst of our coaching, our peer learning, and our vision community, he will draw all the component parts of the process into his life (John 12:32).

Self-Assessment Questions

- Who are the people in your life most interested in your inner growth? What role do they play in that process? Coach? Peer group? Vision community?
- What do you think are the key qualities to look for in a coaching relationship?
- Who are the people who know you intimately, with whom you are free to disclose yourself without having to deal with their reactivity? Who knows what goals you are working on in your life?
- What are two or three new behaviors you would like to see incorporated into your life in significant relationships within your family or congregation?
- How would you distinguish a peer learning group from a personal support group? How would you go about keeping that distinction active in the group's life?

Epilogue

Life in Christ holds a mysterious balance. There are things that only God can do, and there are things that God will not do unless we participate. In this era of societal regression crying out for effective leadership, God has not been awakened from a slumber, wringing his hands over what must be done to address the challenges before us. *He is able* (Ephesians 3:20).

The question that is hanging in the balance is, "Will we participate with God in embracing the transformation that must occur in each of us?" This transformation requires a new set of skills, accompanied by a reflective life of spiritual discipline.

Not many of us can accomplish the task of transformation by working alone. Yielding our lives to Jesus Christ and walking with a community of fellow learners is essential. We have been blessed and encouraged by the emergence of such a community among pastoral and congregational leaders in Houston. It is a community, small but growing, that transcends denomination and culture. In cities across the country, this process is being replicated. In the face of this reality, we must do our part with commitment and urgency.

The Apostle Paul says it clearly: "No prolonged infancies among us, please. We'll not tolerate babes in the woods, small children who are an easy mark for the impostors. God wants us to grow up, to know the whole truth and tell it in love—like Christ in everything. We take our lead from Him, who is the source of everything we do. He keeps us in step with each other. His very breath and blood flow through us, nourishing us so that we will grow up healthy in God, robust in love" (Ephesians 4:13–16, *The Message*).

This is our heartfelt hope for you!

Appendix A: Constructing a Family Diagram

When constructing a family diagram, it is usually helpful to begin with oneself. Draw the appropriate gender symbol and darken the outline so it will stand out from the others you'll draw. Each person in the diagram has a gender symbol along with important information written inside it.

Male Female

Information may include name, age, birth date, occupation, health issues (including mental health), highest level of education, and so on. It may also include idiosyncratic information, such as religious background, job changes, drug and alcohol problems, and the like.

Next, we demonstrate the relationships between people, as follows:

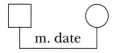

Marriage

Give the date of the marriage (m. date) and dates of separation (s. date) and divorce (div. date). Notice that males are usually on the left and females on the right (in the case of multiple marriages, this rule may be broken).

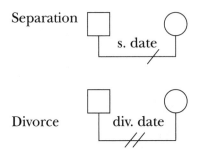

Separation s. date

Divorce div. date

Significant relationship (especially one that produces a child) is also shown:

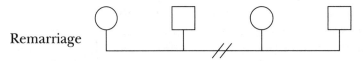

Remarriage

Now we begin to add layers to the diagram by adding children to each generation.

Children are listed in the order of their birth, with the oldest child on the far left and the youngest child on the far right.

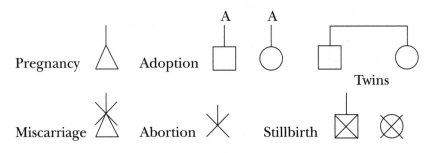

Pregnancy   Adoption   Twins

Miscarriage   Abortion   Stillbirth

Death is indicated by crossing through the gender symbol and adding the date (d. date) and cause of death.

Information about the nature of relationships between family members can also be added. This becomes subjective material and the beginning of interpreting the family system.

Conflict

Cutoff

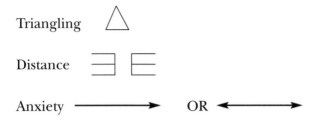

Triangling

Distance

Anxiety ⟶   OR ⟵⟶

Symptoms may be indicated by shading the gender symbol:

The symptoms in question can be identified and described, and the severity can be rated using a scale of 1 to 10.

A family diagram sometimes becomes cluttered and unwieldy. If this happens, some information can be recorded on a separate piece of paper. It may be helpful to use a large piece of paper, to draw a practice sketch first using just the gender symbols and the relationship symbols, and to use more than one color of ink.

When the diagram is completed, we ask these questions (from Kerr and Bowen's *Family Evaluation: An Approach Based on Bowen Theory*):

1. What stressors do we see affecting this family? How does the family react?

2. What do we notice about sibling position? For example, what sibling position does a marriage partner hold (for instance, an oldest daughter marrying a youngest son, and so on)? What do we notice about family size?

3. How do we see the flow of emotional process in the family? Where does the anxiety go? At what level of emotional functioning does the family seem to settle? What forms of reactivity do we see? Where do we see evidence of cutoff? distance? triangling? child focus? conflict?

4. What symptoms developed in the family? Do we see patterns of symptom development? For example, do the symptoms tend to manifest themselves in one gender or the other? Do they tend to be health-related (somatic) or addiction or mental illness?

5. How adaptive is the family? In other words, what is the level of emotional reactivity in comparison to the level of stress the members are experiencing? A high level of emotional reactivity when stress is low is considered a low level of adaptiveness. Conversely, if a family has a reasonably low level of emotional reactivity under a high level of stress, it is considered to be highly adaptive.

For more information about family diagrams, we recommend the works in the Bibliography by Roberta Gilbert (*Connecting with Our Children*), Harriet Lerner, and Monica McGoldrick and Randy Gerson.

Appendix B: An Overview
of Key Spiritual Disciplines

A variety of spiritual disciplines have been practiced by Christians throughout time and around the world. This list is by no means exhaustive and describes only a few of the most common and time-honored ways of seeking God and learning to do his will.

Celebration The discipline of celebration teaches us to focus on the joy of our salvation and on our gratitude for God's good gifts. We replace anxiety and fear with "holy delight and joy" in our response to God's work in our lives (Willard, *The Spirit of the Disciplines*).

Chastity Long misunderstood, chastity is purposeful self-discipline of our sexuality, especially when we deliberately focus our attention away from sexual fulfillment. Chastity is not the same as celibacy and may be practiced by someone who is married (when both partners agree) or single (1 Corinthians 7:1–6).

Confession Radical honesty in fellowship with trusted believers in which we reveal our personal weaknesses and failures, resulting in healing and redemption; sometimes appropriate restitution follows confession (James 5:16).

Fasting The experience of deliberately abstaining from food or some other indulgence to create more space in one's life for attending to God. In fasting, one learns to control various appetites and submit them to God.

Journaling A spiritual journal is a form of focused writing in which the disciple records his or her prayers, impressions, and insights. In a spiritual journal, we reflect on the presence of God in our lives and record what we believe he is saying to us.

Meditation A form of listening to God. It usually involves sustained attention on a single passage of Scripture, a single word, or a single idea. When we meditate, we seek to hear the voice of God and to experience his presence.

Prayer Communication with God, both talking and listening. We set aside a specific time for sustained prayer, and we also learn to talk and listen to God as we go about our normal lives. Prayer is an important part of our practice of all the other disciplines.

Service Serving others in love is a fundamental discipline of the Christian. Servanthood teaches us to follow the example of Jesus by rejecting ego and self-promotion in favor of humbly seeking to meet the practical needs of others.

Silence When we deliberately try to eliminate as many sources of unnecessary noise as possible, we are freed from external distraction and are better able to hear from God and from our own souls. We also forgo the use of words to distract and manipulate others.

Solitude Choosing to withdraw from the company of other people teaches us to be alone with God. Solitude gives us the opportunity to reflect on the pressures of a relationship and our daily lives and reorient ourselves to the will of God.

Spiritual direction The spiritual director becomes a mentor in our spiritual lives. We submit our experiences to the spiritual director, who then guides us in recognizing and responding to God's ever-present activity in our lives. A formal, purposeful relationship, spiritual direction is distinct from counseling and friendship (both of which also have their place in the lives of Christians).

Stewardship When we practice stewardship of our resources, we acknowledge that everything we have belongs to God and has been given to us to be managed responsibly and for his glory. Stewardship includes sharing, giving, and simplicity.

Study As we study, we focus our minds on Scripture or other spiritually helpful literature with the purpose of increasing our learning and understanding. Study involves repetition, concentration, comprehension, and reflection. The goal of study is transformation of the mind.

Worship In worship, we adore God and celebrate his attributes. Whether we worship with other believers or individually, worship focuses on the glory of God and our role in honoring him.

Recommended Reading

For full citations of publisher information, see the Bibliography.

Edwin Friedman, *Generation to Generation: Family Process in Church and Synagogue.*

Friedman was a rabbi and a student of Murray Bowen. This book applies Bowen's systems thinking to the emotional processes at work in the three systems in which a pastor lives and works: the pastor's own family, the families of the congregation, and the family that is the congregation. This book is a must for any pastoral leader attempting to apply family systems thinking to the leader's role.

Edwin Friedman, *A Failure of Nerve: Leadership in the Age of the Quick Fix.*

Friedman died in 1996. Some of his own family and colleagues prepared this incomplete manuscript for publication. In this work, he focused specifically on the nature of leadership in a highly anxious system.

Roberta Gilbert, *Extraordinary Relationships: A New Way of Thinking About Human Interactions.*

Gilbert's book is a very readable primer in understanding Bowen Family Systems Theory. Explanatory diagrams and anecdotes are plentiful. Gilbert is a practicing psychiatrist and a member of the faculty at the Bowen Center for the Study of the Family in Washington, D.C. She also offers leadership training for pastors and managers.

Michael Kerr and Murray Bowen. *Family Evaluation: An Approach Based on Bowen Theory.*

This book is a basic textbook in the study of Bowen Family Systems Theory. It is academic in style, but quite readable. Kerr became the director of the Bowen Center after Dr. Bowen's death in 1990. Readers should note that Murray Bowen and many others who write in this field do so from an evolutionary scientific perspective. The assumptions of evolution are not, in our estimation, necessary for understanding and applying the theory. Intelligent design theory, for example (such as that offered by William A. Dembski and Michael J. Behe in *Intelligent Design: The Bridge Between Science and Theology,* InterVarsity Press, 1999), could account for the same observations.

Harriet G. Lerner, *The Dance of Intimacy.*

This book, along with its companion, *The Dance of Anger,* describes most of the ideas of Bowen Family Systems Theory in a highly readable, engaging style. Although targeted to women, these books are practical and helpful for anyone wanting to use these principles to improve their intimate relationships.

Reggie McNeal, *A Work of Heart: Understanding How God Shapes Spiritual Leaders.*

McNeal is an effective leadership coach who provides, in this work, both a biblical and a practical review of how leaders learn. McNeal examines how the lives of Moses, David, Paul, and Jesus were shaped. He calls leaders to live in learning communities as a primary strategy for effectiveness and longevity.

Ronald W. Richardson, *Creating a Healthier Church: Family Systems Theory, Leadership and Congregational Life.*

In this helpful book, Richardson tells a tale of two churches facing the exact set of circumstances that produce a high level of acute anxiety. One congregation is characterized by a high level of chronic anxiety and has leaders with a low level of emotional maturity. The other has a low level of chronic anxiety and leaders with a high level of emotional maturity. Practically and humorously, Richardson brings the concepts of the living system to life.

Douglas J. Rumford, *SoulShaping: Taking Care of Your Spiritual Life.*

Rumford describes how regular practice of a variety of spiritual disciplines helps us avoid the neglect of our souls and strengthens us for a powerful, Christ-centered spirituality. This is a richly practical book, explaining several spiritual exercises and offering encouragement, guidelines, and questions for reflection and discussion in each chapter.

Peter Senge, *The Fifth Discipline: The Art and Practice of the Learning Organization.*

When Senge wrote this book in 1990, it became a seminal work that has shaped our understanding of leadership in living systems. A highly influential book, it gives the reader tremendous insight into the nature of systems.

Dallas Willard, *The Spirit of the Disciplines: Understanding How God Changes Lives.*

This work is a thoroughgoing examination of the classic disciplines of the Christian faith. It is not so much an overview of the disciplines—although Willard's distinction of disciplines of engagement and disciplines of abstinence is helpful. It is a philosophical and psychological treatment of how the disciplines actually work to form Christ in our bodies. Like many of Willard's books, this is not an easy read, but for those who persevere, the rewards are rich.

Dallas Willard, *The Divine Conspiracy: Rediscovering Our Hidden Life in God.*

Willard brings the gospel to life in an incredibly fresh way in this book reexamining the Sermon on the Mount. He distinguishes church members found in Western culture from the disciples that Jesus calls us to be. This is a challenging, inspiring renewal of the vision of what it means to follow Christ.

Dallas Willard, *Renovation of the Heart: Putting on the Character of Christ.*

In a comprehensive yet readable manner, Willard offers a primer on spiritual formation. He clearly analyzes the human person in all his or her complexities and offers practical guidance on how to help the person be formed in the ways of Christ. This is on the short list of "must reads" for anyone who is interested in the topic of discipleship.

Dallas Willard, *Hearing God.*

Many believe that prayer is among the foundational spiritual disciplines. In this clear, concise text, Willard brings new insights and a fresh hearing to this discipline.

Glossary

Anxiety The emotional and physiological response to a threat that may be either real or perceived.

Anxiety, acute The response we make to threat that is both real and time-limited.

Anxiety, chronic Our reaction to a perceived, imagined, or distorted threat that is not time-limited.

Coach Someone in our lives who plays the role of furnishing an outside angle; someone outside our relationship system who offers a degree of objectivity about our lives and with whom we can consult in our attempt to become more differentiated.

Conflict A common symptom of anxiety in a system, in which people insist on their way as the only way and clash with others taking the same emotional stance.

Creating urgency The intentional act, on the part of a leader, to make clear the tension between current reality and a vision for a preferred future.

Cutoff A common symptom of anxiety in a system, an extreme expression of distancing, in which people completely break off relationships. (See *distancing*)

Detriangling The ability to remain connected to the other two parties in an emotional triangle in a one-to-one relationship, not taking on the anxiety that belongs to the two of them. (See *triangle*)

Differentiation of self A person's capacity to remain true to his or her principles, to be thoughtful rather than reactive, while remaining emotionally connected to others who are important to him or her.

Distancing A common symptom of anxiety in a system, in which people withdraw from others emotionally, creating superficial harmony. (See *cutoff*)

Emotional maturity (See *differentiation of self*)

Emotional process The interaction of the level of differentiation and the level of chronic anxiety; the interplay of the togetherness forces and the autonomy forces, and the emergence of symptoms within a relational system.

Emotional reactivity The automatic, unthinking, emotional response human beings make to a real or perceived threat in their environment. (See *anxiety*)

Emotional system The emotional connectedness that develops when people engage in a relationship that is long-term, intense, and significant.

Emotional triangle See *triangle.*

Emotions As a technical term, "emotions" are not equivalent to "feelings." The term *emotional* refers to all the responses a human being makes to anxiety, most of which are below the level of awareness; it includes our entire physiology (digestion, skin temperature, heart rate, blood pressure, and so on). (See *feelings*)

Family diagram A representation of one's family in which the emotional processes of the family can be charted by use of symbols and abbreviations.

Family of origin The emotional unit in which a person is reared.

Feelings Emotional responses that operate at the level of awareness; emotional responses of which we are conscious. (See *emotions*)

Individuality force The internal pressure we feel to express our individuality, to be for ourselves, to differentiate from others. (See *togetherness force*)

Interlocking triangles The connection of emotional triangles within a relational system, which permits anxiety to travel from one triangle throughout the entire system.

Joharri's window A tool developed by Joe Luft and Harry Ingham to assist a person in increasing self-awareness, on the basis of a matrix of what we know about ourselves and what others know about us.

Leadership The capacity to know and do the right thing in spite of pressure to do something else.

Learning community A set of significant relationships among people who are mutually committed to the transformational journey and who provide a source of objectivity, accountability, and wisdom for one another.

Multigenerational process How a level of emotional maturity and ways of responding to anxiety are transmitted from one generation to the next.

Nuclear family The family in which one lives, which may include husband, wife, and children.

Overfunctioning A common symptom of anxiety in a system, in which one member of the system takes on responsibilities that belong to others. (See *underfunctioning*)

Peer group (See *learning community*)

Process (See *emotional process*)

Projection A common symptom of anxiety in a system, in which a portion or portions of the system focus attention on another part as "the problem"; the part that is focused upon often agrees with this diagnosis. Projection also occurs in conflict, as each person blames the other for the problems in the relationship.

Reactivity (See *emotional reactivity*)

Reflection The discipline of intentionally setting aside time to evaluate one's progress in the transformational journey, comparing one's performance with one's intentions and desires.

Relational system (See *emotional system*)

Shared vision A view of an organization's future that is held in common by key leaders within the system.

Spiritual disciplines Those practices in the spiritual life that one intentionally takes on to experience transformation of life toward greater spiritual maturity.

Sibling position The unique place one occupies in the family of origin, on the basis of one's birth order (oldest, older brother of sisters, younger sister of sisters, and so forth). This position may teach one about relationships with both sexes and affect how one functions in the system. Sibling position does not determine one's behavior, but in many cases it influences behavior, especially as anxiety rises.

Stress (See *anxiety*)

Systems thinking The capacity to see the whole and the parts of a system simultaneously, noticing the contribution made by each person and the effect of each upon the other. This includes the ability to recognize the symptoms of increasing anxiety and to note the part one plays in the system's reactivity.

Thinking systems (See *systems thinking*)

Togetherness force The pressure we experience from important relationships and relationship systems to be "for the system," to conform to others, to fit in. (See *individuality force*)

Triangle The "molecule" of the emotional system, formed when one person becomes uncomfortable in relationship to another and so pulls in a third to manage the anxiety in the original relationship. *Triangling* is the act of forming such a triangle. (See *detriangling*)

Transformation Change in an individual, a church, or a community that alters both the mental model one uses to view the world and one's behavior in the world.

Underfunctioning A common symptom of anxiety in a system, in which a portion or portions of the system fail to accept responsibility for their own functioning, allowing others to take it up for them. (See *overfunctioning*)

Vision community A diverse group of key members of a system who become a committed and trusting community to discern and implement God's vision for the congregation. (See *shared vision*)

Bibliography

Bowen, M. *Family Therapy in Clinical Practice.* Northvale, N.J.: Jason Aronson, 1994.

Buchanan, M. *Your God Is Too Safe: Rediscovering the Wonder of a God You Can't Control.* Sisters, Oreg.: Multnomah, 2001.

Burns, D. *Feeling Good: The New Mood Therapy.* New York: HarperCollins, 1999.

Covey, S. R. *The 7 Habits of Highly Effective Families: Building a Beautiful Family Culture in a Turbulent World.* New York: Golden Books, 1997.

Foster, R. J. *Celebration of Discipline: The Path to Spiritual Growth.* New York: HarperCollins, 1978.

Frankl, V. *Man's Search for Meaning.* Boston: Beacon Press, 1959.

Friedman, E. *Generation to Generation: Family Process in Church and Synagogue.* New York: Guilford Press, 1985.

Friedman, E. *A Failure of Nerve: Leadership in the Age of the Quick Fix.* Bethesda, Md.: Edwin Friedman Estate/Trust, 1999.

Gilbert, R. M. *Extraordinary Relationships: A New Way of Thinking About Human Interactions.* New York: Wiley, 1992.

Gilbert, R. M. *Connecting with Our Children: Guiding Principles for Parents in a Troubled World.* New York: Wiley, 1998.

Graham, B. *Just As I Am.* San Francisco: HarperSanFrancisco, 1997.

Herrington, J., Bonem, M., and Furr, J. *Leading Congregational Change: A Practical Guide for the Transformational Journey.* San Francisco: Jossey-Bass, 2000.

Hybels, B. *Too Busy Not to Pray: Slowing Down to Be with God.* Downers Grove, Ill.: InterVarsity Press, 1988.

Johnson, D. W. *Reaching Out: Interpersonal Effectiveness and Self-Actualization.* (6th ed.) Boston: Allyn and Bacon, 1997.

Kerr, M., and Bowen, M. *Family Evaluation: An Approach Based on Bowen Theory.* New York: Norton, 1988.

Lerner, H. G. *The Dance of Intimacy.* New York: HarperCollins, 1989.

London, H. B., and Wiseman, N. B. *Pastors at Risk: Help for Pastors, Hope for the Church.* Wheaton, Ill.: Victor Books, 1993.

McGoldrick, M., and Gerson, R. *Genograms in Family Assessment.* New York: Norton, 1985.

McNeal, R. *A Work of Heart: Understanding How God Shapes Spiritual Leaders.* San Francisco: Jossey-Bass, 2000.

Nouwen, H. *In the Name of Jesus: Reflections on Christian Leadership.* New York: Crossroad, 1991.

Richardson, R. W. *Creating a Healthier Church: Family Systems Theory, Leadership, and Congregational Life.* Minneapolis: Fortress Press, 1996.

Rumford, D. J. *SoulShaping: Taking Care of Your Spiritual Life.* Wheaton, Ill.: Tyndale, 1996.

Senge, P. *The Fifth Discipline: The Art and Practice of the Learning Organization.* New York: Doubleday, 1990.

Tan, S.-Y., and Gregg, D. H. *Disciplines of the Holy Spirit.* Grand Rapids, Mich.: Zondervan, 1997.

Titelman, P. (ed.). *Clinical Applications of Bowen Family Systems Theory.* New York: Haworth Press, 1998.

Willard, D. *The Spirit of the Disciplines: Understanding How God Changes Lives.* San Francisco: HarperSanFrancisco, 1988.

Willard, D. *The Divine Conspiracy: Rediscovering Our Hidden Life in God.* San Francisco: HarperSanFrancisco, 1998.

Willard, D. *Hearing God.* Downers Grove, Ill.: Intervarsity Press, 1999.

Willard, D. *Renovation of the Heart: Putting on the Character of Christ.* Colorado Springs: NavPress, 2002.

The Authors

Jim Herrington is a pastor, author, and conference leader. He serves as the pastor of Harbor Church, a network of house churches in Houston's Montrose Community. He also serves as the team leader for Mission Houston, an interdenominational ministry committed to transforming the city through a strategically unified and mobilized body of Christ. He holds a master's of religious education degree from Southwestern Baptist Theological Seminary in Fort Worth. He has served as congregational growth/health consultant to more than one thousand pastors and congregations across the United States, with special focus in spiritual renewal, leadership development, and managing change. He is the cofounder of LeadersEdge, a nationally recognized leadership development process for pastoral leaders, based in Houston. Along with James Furr and Mike Bonem, he is the coauthor of *Leading Congregational Change: A Practical Guide for the Transformational Journey* and a contributing author to *City Reaching: On the Road to Community Transformation,* by Jack Dennison. Herrington has been married to Betty, a kindergarten teacher in Houston, for thirty years. They have four children and two grandchildren.

R. Robert Creech has served as the senior pastor of the University Baptist Church in Houston since 1987. He received his Ph.D. from Baylor University in New Testament studies in 1984 and taught on the faculty of Houston Baptist University for seven years. He was involved in developing the LeadersEdge program in Houston and is cofounder of SemiNEXT (www.seminext.org), a program of on-line theological training. He has been married to Melinda for twenty-eight years, and they have three children.

Trisha Taylor is a certified pastoral counselor with the Union Baptist Association Center for Counseling in Houston. She is a Fellow in the American Association of Pastoral Counselors and is licensed as a professional counselor in the state of Texas. She is also on the faculty of LeadersEdge. She holds a bachelor's degree from Baylor University and a master's degree from Southwestern Baptist Theological Seminary. She is active in ministry at Clear Lake Baptist Church, where her husband, Craig, is pastor. They have two children, Andrew and Rebecca.

About Leadership Network

The mission of Leadership Network is to accelerate the effectiveness of the Church by identifying and connecting strategic leaders and providing them with access to resources in the form of new ideas, people, and tools.

Leadership Network's focus has been on the practice and application of faith at the local congregational level. Churches and church leaders served by Leadership Network represent a wide variety of primarily Protestant faith traditions that range from mainline to evangelical to independent. All are characterized by innovation, entrepreneurial leadership, and a desire to be on the leading edge of ministry.

Established as a private foundation in 1984 by social entrepreneur Bob Buford, Leadership Network is acknowledged as an influential leader among churches and faith-based ministries and a major resource to which innovative leaders turn for networking and information.

For additional information on Leadership Network, please contact

Leadership Network
2501 Cedar Springs, Suite 200
Dallas, Texas 75201
800–765–5323
www.leadnet.org

Index